Training in Compassion

# Training in Compassion

*Zen Teachings on the Practice of Lojong*

NORMAN FISCHER

Shambhala
*Boston & London*
2013

Shambhala Publications, Inc.
Horticultural Hall
300 Massachusetts Avenue
Boston, Massachusetts 02115
www.shambhala.com

9 8 7 6 5 4 3 2 1

First Edition
Printed in the United States of America

⊗ This edition is printed on acid-free paper
that meets the American National Standard.
♺ This book is printed on 30% postconsumer recycled paper.
For more information please visit www.shambhala.com.

Distributed in the United States by Random House, Inc.,
and in Canada by Random House of Canada Ltd

Designed by James D. Skatges

Library of Congress Cataloging-in-Publication Data

Fischer, Norman, 1946–
Training in compassion: Zen teachings on the practice
of lojong / Norman Fischer.
    pages   cm
ISBN 978-1-61180-040-1 (pbk.)
1. Blo-sbyon. 2. Zen Buddhism—Doctrines. I. Title.
BQ7805.F57 2013
294.3'444—dc23
2012028231

To my wife, Kathie Fischer, and to the memory of her father, my father-in-law, Donald W. Yockey (1920–2012).

# Contents

# Acknowledgments

This book was made possible by the work of dedicated practitioners in the Everyday Zen sangha who transcribed and edited talks I have given. These include practitioners from Montaña Despierta in Xalapa, Mexico: Alfredo Amescua, Bertha Laura Barrientos Beverido, Gina Lozano, Marcela Lozano, Porfirio Carrillo, Oleg Gorfinkel, Malu Gatti, Paula Busseniers, Eugenia Vignau, Alessandra Barzizza, Gerardo Gonzalez, and Sergio Stern; Barbara Byrum in the San Francisco Bay Area; Russ Russell in Santa Cruz, California; and Murray McGillivray in Calgary, Canada.

# Introduction

Times are tough. We live fast-paced lives, with considerable political, economic, and ecological upheaval, and the resultant dread, fear, and stress make life difficult for almost everyone—except, possibly, those who opt for self-defensive denial, which only defers the pain and probably makes it worse.

But times have always been tough. Living a human life, in a human world, on a limited planet, has always been a daunting proposition. Circling the wagons, assuming a self-centered defensive stance, has never been a successful coping mechanism, natural though the impulse may be. We are programmed by evolution in the opposite way: we are cooperating animals, deeply conditioned to be concerned for one another. Our hearts are made for loving.

Compassion and connection not only feel good and right (as all of our religious traditions teach us), they also turn difficulties into opportunities—as we have seen so often when, in the course of the seemingly more frequent natural disasters of recent years, neighbors go out of their way to help one another. When they do, tragedy becomes inspirational. Paradoxically, life can seem more, rather than less, meaningful when our world is suddenly shattered. When we are witness to genuine compassion in the face of great suffering, we seem to transcend our difficulties. When we feel like helping, do help, and are helped, we become stronger, happier, more resilient people.

Compassion and resilience are not, as we might imagine, rarified human qualities available only to the saintly. Nor are they adventitious experiences that arise in us only in extraordinary circumstances. In fact, these essential and universally prized human qualities can be solidly cultivated by anyone willing to take the time to do it. They can become the way we are and live on a daily basis. We can train our minds. We are not stuck with our fearful, habitual, self-centered ways of seeing and feeling.

## How Can We Train the Mind?

Mind, as I mean it in this book, is more than intellect. It also includes sensations, emotions, subtle senses of subjectivity, desires, aspirations, attitudes, images, concepts, perceptions, and so on. In a word, mind is consciousness, the sum total of our human experience. In this sense, mind also includes body—we are conscious of our bodily sensations, and our emotions, maybe our thoughts too, affect us bodily and vice versa.

Most of us think of our minds, "the way we are," our basic attitudes and reactions, as being fixed by our genetic inheritance and life experience. We assume that our basic feelings and reactions are simply a given, indelibly fixed in us. We can learn information and specific skills, which is why we go to school or invest in training programs. Yet our basic character remains the same. If we're genetically or environmentally programmed to be angry, sad, depressed, or cheerful people, we will continue to be that way more or less throughout our lives. We are who we are.

But contemporary cognitive science is proving this assumption false. In fact, our minds, our character, our patterns of thought and emotion, are much more fluid than we thought they were. Our brains are renewed through activity and reflection; they are, as scientists say, plastic. So our minds are trainable. Our basic patterns of thought and feeling can be different. This is news we are only now in the process of fully digesting.

For most of us, our default untrained mind isn't very inspired. We are easily discouraged, distracted, offended, or hurt. When things don't go well, when life presents us with great or grave challenges, we are more likely to wilt or whine than to rise to the occasion. Our horizons are severely limited. We want to be successful and accomplished, but the smallness of our self-confidence stops us in our tracks. Or maybe we *are* accomplished, but it's not enough to satisfy our inner need. We want to love and be loved, but because of our bruised egos and checkered pasts, love doesn't come easily or naturally. Even lives that seem outwardly to be happy and full can feel lonely and unfulfilled on the inside. And when, on the other hand, we report that we are content with our lives, it may well be because we have sets our sights too low. We haven't touched the great possibilities, haven't even considered that we could love widely and absolutely, that we could be compassionate, wise, deep, appreciative, and resilient people. Most of us in these cynical and embattled times don't consider such things as even remotely within our grasp. We feel lucky simply not to be struggling.

But much more than this is possible. We know that if we want to develop stamina and strength in the body, we have to work at it steadily and repeatedly over time. It won't do to simply decide we are going to do weight training, read a book about it, and intend to do it. The reading, the thinking, the intention, would only be a beginning. We'd need to go to the gym and do our reps, and keep that up over time. This is true for the mind as well—training the mind takes not only know-how and intention, it also takes repetitive training over time.

This is where the whole apparatus of spiritual practice with its many techniques comes in.

Spiritual practice, exactly like training in a gym, takes time and effort. Just as there are stationary bicycles, treadmills, weight machines, and other devices, so in spiritual practice there is prayer, meditation, ritual, study, and other techniques. Using these steadily over time, we can change our minds. We can begin to notice our unsuccessful repetitive patterns of thinking and feeling. We can begin to see their consequences. We can stop unconsciously identifying with them, as if they defined us, and go beyond grief and self-blame to a sense of curiosity and hopefulness. We can begin to cultivate new ways of thinking, feeling, speaking, and acting and gradually make them more and more our own. Our basic patterns over time will be different as we train our minds with intentional techniques and practices, and this will influence our relationships and our sense of ourselves and the world.

The traditional text on which this book is based, translated usually as *The Root Text of the Seven Points of Training the Mind* (often called, for short, *Lojong* in Tibetan), is one of the greatest texts for training the mind in all of world religion. Its seven key points are further subdivided into fifty-nine slogans. The original text was composed in Tibet in the twelfth century (for some reason a particularly fruitful period in world religion—the time, more or less, of Aquinas, Maimonides, Averroes, and Dogen, among many others) by Geshe Chekawa Yeshe Dorje. It's based on an earlier fifty-nine-slogan text of the tenth-century Indian master Atisha. Throughout Tibetan Buddhist history, up to the present, masters have lectured on and written commentaries to this text, using it as the basis for practical hands-on training in the cultivation of compassion and resilience. Its popularity in Asia has transferred to the West, where today the text is studied by many Buddhist teachers, who have begun writing their own commentaries to make mind training readily available to their students. Traditional commentaries in English include Ken McLeod's translation of a seminal commentary by the Tibetan master Jamgon Kongtrul, under the title *The Great Path of Awakening*. The storied Tibetan master Dilgo Khyentse Rinpoche's commentary is available as *Enlightened Courage*. There are contemporary Western commentaries by the great and colorful twentieth-century Tibetan Buddhist founder Chögyam Trungpa, and by his disciple the nun Pema Chödrön, whom I have been fortunate enough to know and practice with. There is scholar-practitioner B. Alan Wallace's *Buddhism with an Attitude: The Tibetan Seven-Point Mind-Training*. And many more. (For the wording of the slogans in this book, I have relied mainly on Chögyam Trungpa's lively renderings into English—also used by Pema Chödrön—and, where I felt it necessary for the points I wanted to emphasize, have made my own versions.)

## Why Another Commentary?

There are three reasons for this commentary: First, a great and relevant text for spiritual practice deserves as many commentaries by as many voices as possible. Each new commentary inevitably adds some refreshment, showing overlooked angles for practice.

Second, because I am a Zen Buddhist priest who has studied Tibetan and Theravadin Buddhism as well as Western religious traditions, there is a good chance that my Zen perspective on an Indo-Tibetan Buddhist text will be different in some advantageous ways. This is often the case with cross-traditional religious studies. I have experienced this before. One of my previous books is *Opening to You: Zen-Inspired Translations of the Psalms,* which, judging from the comments of many readers over the years, has had value for Jewish and Christian readers already quite familiar with the psalms. Somehow, my "outsider's view" shed new light for many readers on these beautiful ancient texts.

Another reason a specifically Zen approach to a non-Zen text might be worthwhile has to do with a characteristic of Zen itself: its commonsense simplicity. Religion in general and Buddhism in particular can be pretty complicated. Although Buddhism may now appear in Western culture as a fresh breeze, the truth is Buddhism throughout Asian history has had all the upsides and downsides of any religion. It has been just as tradition-bound and scholastic as any religion gets to be over time. Zen's original formation in China was a reaction to this very tendency. Although in time Zen, too, became elaborated and ritualized, the basic Zen impulse is to avoid piety and cut directly to the chase. Its language and methodology is iconoclastic and plainspoken. Possibly such an attitude will do this old text some good.

The third reason for this commentary has to do with what I consider a serious weakness in Zen: its deficiency in explicit teachings on compassion.

Zen is a school of Mahayana Buddhism, and like all Mahayana schools, compassion is its foundation. Yet most Zen literature and lore appears to be rough, theoretical (in an antitheoretical way), and austere (if often humorous). Since Zen is so fixated on cutting through complications and focusing on a few simple, profound points, it assumes rather than encourages compassion and has very little to say about it. This is why I have taken to presenting the Indo-Tibetan teachings on compassion and altruism in my Zen retreats and seminars and have made them a part of my personal Zen curriculum. They fill in the gaps, for Western students, that Zen leaves. And since no other text that I know of, in any tradition, is as thoroughgoing and as systematic as the Seven Points in speaking of the practical cultivation of compassion and resilience, it seems to me worthwhile not only for Zen practitioners but for all students of religion and spirituality to have a commentary to it that opens it out a bit from the context of its original traditional setting.

Another thing: it is particularly important to me, after a lifetime devoted to religious practice, to remember that religion is supposed to be a path for full human development, not, as it too often seems to be, a restrictive and narrow-minded ideology that makes you feel as if you have an exclusive purchase on the truth. Interreligious sharing has been a part of my practice for many years, and through it I have learned that if we human beings want to survive with any graciousness on this planet, we need to affirm and share each other's religious practice rather than continue to use religion as a way to further divide us (and I include values-based atheism and secularism as forms of religion for those who find conventional religious symbolism and practice meaningless, offensive, or wounding). It is an odd and disturbing fact that although all religions teach love and compassion, religion throughout history has probably generated at least as much exclusivity and violence as love. Probably more. So I am sympathetic to those who feel that religion should be abandoned altogether or somehow denatured into a diffuse spirituality, without being "organized." And yet there is tremendous know-how and wisdom in our great religious traditions. It would be a shame to give that up, even if we could. I am sure that giving ourselves permission to study and practice with each others' sacred texts and teachings will help to soften and release religion's exclusivity and narrowness. Since it is very likely that religion is not going to go away any time soon, it is better to work with it than to ignore it.

## A Word about Slogans

Like bumper stickers or advertising taglines, slogans are short, punchy phrases that make an immediate impression. Like a catchy tune, they are easy to remember, think about, and stay with.

The best way to develop a mind-training slogan is to work with it initially on your meditation cushion (see basic meditation instructions in appendix 2). The technique is simple enough: sitting calmly with breath and body awareness, simply repeat the slogan silently to yourself again and again, reflect lightly on it, breathe it in with the inhale, out with the exhale. The point is not to sit and think about the slogan as much as to develop it as an almost physical object, a feeling in your belly or heart. Doing this repeatedly will fix it in your mind at a level deeper than is possible with ordinary distracted thinking.

After this initial fixing of the slogan in the mind, you can think about it more, journal about it, talk about it with friends, write it down, repeat it to yourself—maybe when you are walking or driving, or any time you remember to do it—committing yourself to holding it in your mind during the day as often as you can. You can post it on your refrigerator, float it across your computer screen. When you suddenly notice you have forgotten it and your mind is muffled with anxiety or worried rumination, use the very moment of forgetting as a cue to remembering rather than as a chance for self-judgment. This is, after all, mind training. Of course you are going to forget! But noticing that you forgot is already remembering. Mind training requires commitment, repetition, and lots of patience.

If you practice with a slogan in this way, soon it will pop into your mind unbidden at various times during the day. Hundreds of times a day instances will arise that seem germane to the slogan you are working with. In this way, you can practice a slogan until it becomes part of your mind—your own thought, a theme for daily living.

Which slogan to practice with and how long to stay with any one slogan? Be serious, attentive, and flexible. It is most important to keep the practice lively—disciplined but lively. Approaching the slogans systematically and in the order given in the book may not always serve. Read the book sequentially, but rather than dutifully beginning to practice with the slogans in order, it may be best to pick a slogan that jumps out at you for some reason, one that seems particularly relevant for the conditions of your life right now, even if you don't know exactly why. And once you find a slogan you want to work with, stay with it for a while—weeks, months, even years. You will find staying with one slogan over time surprising: the meaning and flavor of the slogan will change as events of your life develop, as time advances and the seasons change. It may yield a surprising variety of insights. So it is sometimes good to stay with a slogan even when you feel restless and want to move on. On the other hand, staying with one slogan too long, and too doggedly, will be counterproductive and discouraging. Especially when another slogan calls out to you. A few weeks may in most cases be enough, unless you are inspired to go on longer. And, of course, it is perfectly okay, and recommended, to come back to a slogan you've already worked on. It will certainly yield new insights the second, third, or fourth time around.

Working with phrases is an ancient technique for mind training in almost all literate cultures. In serious Jewish, Muslim, and Christian practice, as well as many versions of Buddhism, texts are chanted daily. They are also studied, memorized, and used as sacred instruction to shape and illuminate conduct and thought. Understood as the word of God (or Buddha), such texts are not to be taken lightly or at face value. There is always more meaning than meets the eye. With this spirit, a line from a prayer or psalm can become a slogan either intentionally or spontaneously, a living treasure for the practitioner, as if the words were a gift for you alone. In early Buddhism the many lists of positive and negative qualities to be developed or abandoned were memorized and used for repetitive practice, and in Zen there is the technique of meditating on a koan, a brief Zen story, that is often, for practice purposes, reduced to a phrase or two. Although the Indo-Tibetan practice of slogans is perhaps more psychological and intentional than these and other practices, it is in its essentials quite similar.

The slogans offered in this book are somewhat unusual in one particular. The reader might notice rather quickly that there is something counterintuitive about their fundamental stance. Ordinarily when confronted with the unpleasant, the troublesome, or the difficult, whether in a situation, a person, or a feeling, the natural impulse is avoidance. We either deny the difficulty (often quite sincerely) or, if we can't deny it, try to ignore it, get rid of it, or escape from it somehow. This seems natural enough. Most people don't thrive on trouble or enjoy unpleasantness. So naturally we approach the slogans in the hope that training in them will help us eliminate difficulties.

But the slogans take exactly the opposite approach. When difficulty arises, the slogans say over and over again, turn toward it rather than away. Although this is not what we want to do, the truth is it's the best way. Turning toward the difficulty will not only make it easier on us in the end, it will also effect the rather astonishing feat of turning the difficulty into a benefit. When we train our mind to embrace what's hard instead of trying to get rid of it, we have begun to walk a path of growth, happiness, and true resilience. Our very difficulties and sufferings, if we hold them the right way, can be wedges to pry open our smallness. This is what the slogans propose. Changing the habit of avoiding difficulty to the habit of engaging it creatively may be the single most important factor for training the mind.

Compassion literally means embracing the suffering of others. To embrace the suffering of others is to be liberated and opened by that suffering, to the point of finding love. But compassion is impossible if we can't learn to bear our own sufferings and difficulties, if our old habit of denying and running away continues to have its way with us. So the practice of mind training begins with the effort to turn toward difficulty rather than away from it. When we are no longer daunted by difficulties but are willing to engage and make use of them, we become truly resilient individuals.

I can imagine many possible way to make use of this book. As with any book, you could read it, enjoy it (at least I hope so), and be influenced by it in whatever way you spontaneously are or are not. No author could expect more than this from a reader. But it is also possible, since this book is essentially a training manual, a course of study, to read it more slowly and more intentionally than you read most books. You could do as I have suggested above—practice with the fifty-nine slogans, reflect on them, meditate on them, read the relevant sections of the book repeatedly and test out what's said against your own experience. You could convene a group to work on the practices with you—or suggest to a group you already belong to that training in the fifty-nine slogans might be a fruitful way to spend some time, possibly even years. I have contemplated the slogans with enjoyment and much personal transformation ever since I first encountered them and have shared them with many people over the years in seminars and retreats in many places, where they have always been well received. It was because of these many warm receptions, and students' desire to see my oral presentations in written form, that I decided to take the time to write this book. However you decide to make use of it, my hope is that the experience will be of benefit not only to you but to your friends and family and, ultimately, to everyone.

In the traditional text, the fifty-nine slogans are organized into seven points that form the structure of the chapters that follow:

1. Resolve to begin
2. Train in empathy and compassion (absolute and relative compassion)
3. Transform bad circumstances into the path
4. Make practice your whole life
5. Assess and extend
6. The discipline of relationship
7. Living with ease in a crazy world

# 1

## Resolve to Begin

THE FIRST POINT OF ZEN mind training includes only one slogan:

### 1. Train in the preliminaries.

You can understand and practice this slogan three ways.

First, *the preliminaries* includes everything difficult that has happened in your life up until the moment you begin the training. The divorce you are going through or have gone through but never digested, the inexplicable breakup from out of the blue, the unexpected death of someone close to you that has shaken you to the core, a terrible childhood you might have thought you'd gotten over but now realize you haven't, an illness, a job loss, or some other present or past disaster may be the preliminaries for you. The difference between just suffering these things and trying to cope and "training" has to do with how you view them, with your sense of resolve and personal responsibility. Even if what happened to you was not your fault, taking responsibility for it now that it has happened, owning it as the stuff of your present life—rather than seeing it as a tragedy that shouldn't have happened and that therefore there's someone to blame (even if there *is* someone to blame) or bemoaning your sad fate and life's terrible injustice—is **Training in the preliminaries**. In other words, to **Train in the preliminaries** is to stop moaning and feeling sorry for yourself and to recognize instead that regardless of what has happened or why, this is your life and you are the only one equipped to deal with it.

And then, based on that sense of personal responsibility, **Training in the preliminaries** involves reflecting on your life so that you can develop the resolve and courage to begin a new life path. **Training in the preliminaries** is the process of looking honestly at your life and making a firm decision to embark on a disciplined spiritual path.

There are many ways to go about this. In Alcoholics Anonymous and other recovery programs, it's done by coming together in community and telling and listening to one another's stories. It can be done with psychotherapy, with journaling or other forms of writing or art, or with any other form of reflective exercise designed intentionally as a format for such training. The point is that you begin by marking a pause in your life, a time when you say to yourself, "The old path is no good anymore. I have come to the end of it. I need to take the time now to review my life so that I can find the motivation to go ahead differently."

Once you take that time and find that motivation, you have trained in the preliminaries.

A friend of mine, a lawyer, had to **Train in the preliminaries** the hard way. After years of toughing out a life full of anger and aggression (he was a plaintiff's trial attorney, suing on behalf of people who had been in terrible accidents, so he had plenty to be angry about), he was depleted, lonely, and lost. At just that moment he experienced a sudden death in his family and then severe marital problems. It was too much for him. He fell into a deep depression and had to be hospitalized—not once but twice.

In the hospital his work in psychotherapy gave him a way to look at his life from another angle. He began to be able to share his story, first with his therapist and then with other people, rather than keeping his inner situation hidden—from himself as well as everyone else, as he had always done: indeed, as he had been trained to do in his family and in law school. He began to see that he could understand his life as a difficult journey rather than as a shameful failure. Yes, he'd gone down, very far down. But down is part of the journey. From that point on, little by little, he began to recover and to make a life path out of helping other lawyers in his situation.

A second way to understand **Train in the preliminaries,** and the way that a Zen student would be most likely to see it, is "practice *zazen* (Zen meditation)." Start a meditation practice, a daily practice if possible, and trust that sitting regularly on your cushion with your breathing and the feeling of your body (as described in appendix 2) will provide the spiritual inspiration and force necessary to set a new process in motion in your life.

A third way is to follow the set of traditional reflections given in Tibetan and Mahayana Buddhism, specifically as a way of **Training in the preliminaries.** There are four key points to think about. If you really take these points seriously, if you think about them long enough and hard enough to see how true they really are, it will change your outlook on life, and you will have found the motivation to begin again. The practice of reflecting on the four points might involve, first, reading about them; second, reading about them again and again; third, writing them down and thinking about them; fourth, journaling about them; and fifth, continuing to bring them up in your meditation practice or other times set aside for personal reflection.

Here are the four points:

First, *The rarity and preciousness of human life.*

Something desirable is even more desirable if it is rare. Its rarity makes it all the more precious and valuable. There are more than seven billion human beings on planet Earth, and this seems like a lot. But maybe not. The earth may contain seven billion or so humans, but it also contains many other living creatures. For instance, every human body is host to trillions of living beings— various kinds of bacteria, mites, and other microscopic creatures that are, in their time and space scale, just as alive and just as vivid as we are in ours. Beyond these trillions (multiplied by seven billion) who live in and on our bodies, there are of course many other larger creatures, creatures we can see and relate to. The number of ants alone, in their various species, is incomparably larger than seven billion, not to mention all the other sorts of insects and other animals that exist in the air and water and on land. If you consider, then, the total number of nonhuman living beings on the earth and could somehow relate that number (though no doubt it is far too large to compute in any meaningful way) to the number of human beings, you would certainly see that human life on earth is a very rare thing. You would have to pick over trillions upon trillions of living creatures before you would find one that was human. And this calculation only involves the planet Earth, this tiny water- and soil-laced planet spinning around a small star within a vast universe. Who knows how many other planets out there have life-forms. Or no life-forms. Therefore, it is no exaggeration to say that human life is not only, as we would all agree anyway, precious and sacred and not to be taken lightly; it is also, in the grand scheme of things, unbelievably rare.

Therefore, your living body is a fortunate, rare, and precious gift, and your human mind—consciousness risen to the point where there can be identity and value and thought and beauty and autonomous choice—is dear beyond compare. Having received this rare and precious gift, how is it that up to now you haven't thought about the best and highest way of fulfilling your human purpose, you haven't resolved to go beyond your self-centeredness and self-concern so that you can begin to manifest wisdom and compassion—or whatever you consider to be the highest of human purposes? Considering deeply the precious-ness of human life, you feel inspired to begin to do something more with your life.

This is the first point to think about, and it is a pleasant, an awesome thing to think about.

The next three points are also awesome but less pleasant.

Second: *The absolute inevitability of death.*

Most of us somehow believe that we are the sole exception to the otherwise universal rule that all living creatures die. We have seen others die, so we know that others die, and if asked we will answer that yes, we do understand that we will die, but somehow, despite this, in our heart of hearts, in our thoughts and feelings, we don't really believe it. Check yourself sometime during the day and ask yourself honestly whether right now, in this moment, you truly believe that you are going to die some-day. The likelihood is that you would have to answer no, at that moment you do not really believe it, you feel as if you are here and are always going to be here.

Yet the reality of death is the most important factor of every moment of our lives, because it's thanks to death that we can cross over from one moment to the next. If this moment doesn't die, totally disappearing, we can't have the next moment. So loss and death are facts of life every moment. But one day a moment will come like all others but different in one respect: it will not be succeeded by another moment. "Oh, he died," people will say then.

One of the disturbing things about this moment is that you never know when it will come. Most of us believe we don't have to worry about this moment because death comes in old age, and since we are not now so old, it's not a problem for us. But death doesn't come only in old age, it comes at any age, and nobody knows when. And even if it were to come in old age, old age comes much more quickly than you thought it would: you were young, you blinked your eyes, thirty or forty years flew by, and now you are no longer young. How did that happen all of a sudden?

Lived time is not uniform and fixed. It is not a substance measured evenly by clocks. In fact, time is subjective. As you grow older, time speeds up. To an infant, a day or a week is an eternity—so much experiencing and learning is going on that time crawls by, almost as if there were no time. To a child beginning summer vacation, the two or three months ahead seem endless, the start of school in the fall a century away. But the older you get, the shorter a month gets. To a middle-aged person, five years goes by rather quickly. Time actually speeds up with age and the accumulation of lived experience. This means that if you are thirty, your life is much more than a third gone: it is maybe 80 percent gone. If you are fifty, is it 95 percent gone. There's not nearly as much time left as you thought there was.

This is a serious problem, and it's a problem now, not later. We ought to recognize that we are in an urgent situation. We have much less time left than we thought, and we have no idea when our lives will end, so it is important that right now we turn our attention to what really matters, that we don't waste time.

The inevitability of death and the scarcity of time are the second point to think about if we want to develop firm motivation for changing our lives.

Third: *The awesome and indelible power of our actions.*

In Buddhism this is called karma, which is not mystical or fatalistic. Karma simply means that each of our actions produces a result. And this means *every* action, both large and small. All of our thoughts, words, and deeds have consequences, and we may never know the measure of these consequences though they are extensive and powerful. In other words, every moment of our lives up to this moment, in which you are holding a book in your hands, with whatever degree of seriousness of intention you have been able to muster—every moment so far in our lives, we have been affecting the world in some subtle yet real way; every moment, we have been participating in creating the world that now exists for ourselves and others. Everything in our lives is important. Everything matters. There are no trivial throwaway moments.

Most of us think of ourselves as rather inconsequential people. We don't take our own power very seriously. Maybe we think the president is important or the mayor is important or the Nobel Prize winner is important, the pop star is important, the Buddhist master is important, but we are not important. But this is not so. The actions, thoughts, and words of each of us are important. All of us together are making the world. So we have to ask ourselves: "How am I living? What kind of actions am I taking? Am I a force for good in the world or am I just another person doing nothing to help and therefore making things worse?" And if we ask these questions seriously, we will have to conclude that we can do much, much better and that we have to do better—that there is no excuse not to and that to do better is an urgent necessity.

Fourth: *The inescapability of suffering.*

Although we don't like to think about it, it seems that sorrow and suffering are inevitable in any human life, even a happy one. There's the suffering of loss, of disappointment, of disrespect; the suffering of physical pain, illness, old age; the suffering of broken relationships, of wanting something badly and not being able to have it, or not wanting something and being stuck with it. There's the inevitable suffering of painful, afflictive emotions, like jealousy, grief, anger, hatred, confusion, anguish—all kinds of emotions that cause suffering. These things are part of life. No one can avoid suffering. Given that this is so, how can we not take our lives in hand and make a serious effort to develop wisdom, compassion, and resilience? How can we not prepare our minds and hearts for the inevitable suffering that we are going to be facing someday? We have insurance for our car or home because we know we need to protect ourselves from the possibility of accident and loss. We go to the doctor because we know our health requires protection. Why then would we not think to guard and strengthen our mind and heart to cope with the suffering that certainly will be coming in some measure at some time? How can we have been so foolish as to have ignored this necessity for so long?

Deep and systematic reflection on these four points constitutes **Training in the preliminaries:**

*The rarity and preciousness of human life.*
*The inevitability of death.*
*The awesome and indelible power of our actions.*
*The inescapability of suffering.*

With this reflection we'll realize that the only adequate response to the sober realities of our lives is some form of spiritual practice. I am not necessarily speaking of religion or spirituality in the conventional sense but, rather, that these reflections will cause us to appreciate the seriousness of our human condition and to recognize that we have to live as seriously as we possibly can in response to the gift and the problem that is our life.

## 2

# Train in Empathy and Compassion

### PART I: *Absolute Compassion*

ASSUMING THAT WE HAVE now spent some time reflecting on our lives and have realized that the time has come to be serious, and maybe have established a meditation practice or some other form of spiritual cultivation, we are ready to go on to the second point of mind training, **Training in empathy and compassion**.

Before we launch into this deep and moving study, let me offer a word of caution: this material is not easy to appreciate. It amounts to a contemplation of Buddhism's most profound teachings, the teachings on emptiness, which more or less correspond, in Western thought, to theology: reflections on the nature of God, not necessarily everyone's cup of tea. Although in general, mind training is very practical and down-to-earth, this particular part of it (unlike the parts that follow) seems not to offer much specific and useful advice on how to extend compassion in the world. Instead it asks, in effect, "What is the world? What is self? What is other?" It engages metaphysical questions.

In considering how to organize this book, I wondered whether this more philosophical section might not be better at the end rather than at the beginning. And I wondered why the sages of old had put it first. Was it just a habit, a tradition, that had gotten started someplace and then just continued? Was there a good reason for it?

I have concluded that there is a good reason for it. If the basis on which we establish compassion is shaky, all of our efforts to change our way of thinking and behaving will also be shaky. If our basic sense of what we and others and the world are isn't clear and accurate, if our fundamental assumptions are false, we won't be able to proceed successfully to change our deeply ingrained habits. So it does turn out that we do need to begin by contemplating the profound nature of self and other. Because if you change the leaves and branches but leave the roots intact, you run the risk of reverting to type.

So it is important to contemplate these difficult teachings at this point, with this caveat: Though I am trying my best to make what follows understandable, don't worry if it leaves you wondering. It is not necessary at this point that you fully embrace these ideas. You only need to have a preliminary sense of them for now. You can come back to them later. You could even, if you want, skip them entirely for now and go on to chapter 4.

Let's begin with considering what *empathy* and *compassion* actually mean.

In English there are at least three words that describe the capacity to feel the feelings of others. *Empathy* is the capacity to feel another's feelings. It requires that we not be so self-absorbed that we're tone-deaf to the experience of others. Most of us, unfortunately and without realizing it, are living the old joke, "Okay, enough about me; let's talk about what *you* think about me." In other words, we are able to feel the feelings of others only insofar as we imagine those feelings have to do with us. Does she like me? Was he offended by what I just said? Is she jealous of me, out to get me, in love with me? This is not empathy at all. Real empathy requires that we develop the capacity to put our own concerns aside long enough to notice what someone else is going through internally, without reference to ourselves.

But empathy doesn't necessarily mean we care. We can be good at sensing what people are feeling just enough to be able to control or manipulate them. Sociopaths and con artists are quite empathetic, uncanny in their ability to feel the feelings of others. Sympathy, on the other hand, is empathy plus caring. When we're sympathetic to others, we want them to be happy and well, we don't want them to be upset or unhappy. We actually care about them. Compassion is sympathy for others specifically in the case of their suffering. Although it is uncomfortable, we are willing to feel the suffering of others and to do something about it when we can, even if all we can do is be with them.

The training suggested in this second point of mind training is the cultivation of all three of these capacities: empathy, sympathy, and compassion. The technical term for this training in Mahayana Buddhism is development of *bodhicitta,* which means, literally, the impulse or desire for spiritual awakening. This doesn't sound much like compassion or sympathy. Yet implicit in the Mahayana Buddhist understanding of spiritual awakening is the thought that spiritual awakening *means* awakening to a heartfelt concern for others, since any selfish effort, even with a goal of wisdom or enlightenment for one's self, would never lead to real awakening; it would always lead to more narrowness. Spiritual awakening is exactly dropping the sense of one's narrow separateness; it is essentially and profoundly altruistic. So cultivating bodhicitta means cultivating true and heartfelt concern for others in a way that is not clingy or arrogant but is based on the accurate wisdom that none of us is alone, we all need each other and are closely related to each other. As they say in Japanese Zen, "We all belong to the same nose hole society."

In our culture, intelligence and caring seem to be quite different from each other. A highly intelligent person may often be a little arrogant or abstract; a deeply feeling person may appear to be a fuzzy thinker. But in Buddhist thought true intelligence and real caring always go together. They are like the two wings of a noble bird that must be activated together in flight, in perfect harmony and rhythm. Buddhism assumes that true intelligence and true altruism always merge.

To be sure, Western culture and religion also value empathy, sympathy, and compassion, as all human beings do, but we do not link these feelings to intelligence and we have no concept that one could train in them. We take it for granted that we will be capable of caring or we won't, depending on our personal character and upbringing, and that if we are not capable of it now, perhaps we will at some point in our lives be inspired or turned around by something that happens to us, or by a person who influences us, and will suddenly see the light. While Buddhism certainly appreciates such possibilities, it adds to them the sense that the impulse to altruism if absent can be encouraged to appear, and if present, can be extended and strengthened with training.

The essence of bodhicitta is, as I have said, love and concern for others. Because of the preliminary reflections that we talked about, we recognize that we really do have to awaken and change our lives. We realize how dangerous and painful life is if we don't open up. We know we have to do it. And as soon as we start to try, we realize immediately that there is no way that we could ever do this alone, because opening up means opening to what's around us, to others, to the world, and to our radical connectedness. Bodhicitta is the feeling of love based on the deep recognition that what we call "self" and what we call "others" are designations, concepts, habits of mind, not realities of the world.

Real altruism isn't self-sacrifice for the benefit of others, a guilt-driven sense that we *should* be good, we *should* be nice, we *should* be kind. It is the profound recognition that self and other are not fundamentally different, only apparently different. Because of this the range of activity and feeling of bodhicitta is much wider than we would expect. A whole world of altruism and its effects opens up before us. We now see that the only way that we could love ourselves is by loving others, and the only way that we could truly love others is to love ourselves. The difference between self-love and love of others is very small, once we really understand. Taking this truth into our hearts and actions is truly life changing. And once we open to it, it becomes impossible to go back. It becomes impossible to fool ourselves anymore with selfishness and resentment. To be sure, we will probably still have plenty of selfish and resentful feelings, but now we know them for what they are, and they are far less compelling, because we have seen for ourselves how stupid, how childish and blind such feelings actually are. And they wouldn't be so bad if they weren't also so painful. But they are. Self-centeredness and all the emotions that flow from it—envy, anger, greed, and so on—are painful. And we no longer feel compelled to go on feeling pain for stupid reasons. We have seen through those reasons. So it becomes almost impossible to be willfully, intentionally aggressive, almost impossible to be willfully, intentionally disrespectful of others, because we can simply see with our eyes, just as we can see the sky above and the sun when it sets, that all of life is one sky warmed by one sun. To separate self from other is simply not in accord with what we see. So there is no way to be resentful, hateful, or self-centered, favoring ourself over others. Even though, because of long habit, we may still be resentful and so on, we know better in our heart of hearts. We see that love isn't an emotional option, it's a fact of life—a fact we know we desperately need to conform to for our own good and happiness. This is a far deeper change of heart than the conventional resolution to be "good" or "nice," though of course it will probably cause us to be better, nicer people. It's a much more raw, visceral, and intimate response.

This gives some notion of how bodhicitta is understood and prized in Mahayana Buddhism. It is considered the most valuable of all insights and is discussed and taught extensively. Of all the schools of Buddhism that have been transmitted to the West, none surpasses the Tibetan Buddhist schools in their immense lexicon of teachings on bodhicitta.

There are nine mind-training slogans under this important second point. The nine are divided into two categories, *absolute bodhicitta* and *relative bodhicitta*.

Absolute bodhicitta is absolute love, love that's bigger than any emotion, bigger than any object, so big that there is no lover and no beloved (the two merge into one under absolute love's force). Love that amounts to a total vision of life as love itself. Within such love there can be no loss, because this love is so big it includes everything—even absence—so that nothing can ever be lost. Absolute bodhicitta is the empty, perfect, expansive, joyful, spacious nature of existence itself. Nor is it something that we have added on to existence. It's always been there in life, as life; it's always been the nature of how things are. Love has been there all along, but we've been so convinced by our smallness that we have failed to look around and notice it. Maybe we could say that absolute bodhicitta is like God, who is always present everywhere, even in absence, and that our awakening to absolute bodhicitta is our coming to know that there is nothing but God and there never was anything but God and there never will be anything but God, and that everything is always held and always has been held, and that we are always loved and have always been loved and so has everything and everyone always been loved.

In contrast to this exalted state and exalted view, *relative bodhicitta* involves our doing a bit of work. Relative bodhicitta is when I roll up my sleeves and get on with the business of actually loving somebody. Relative bodhicitta is when I try to do something, to help somehow, to offer encouragement, support, food, clothing, better laws, improved political systems, and so on. With relative bodhicitta we make efforts that we are successful at or unsuccessful at, we suffer losses and cry over those losses, our hearts are broken and we grieve, or we take delight in our own delight and the delight of others. With relative bodhicitta we try to defend our friends and help people in need. There is no end to the work demanded by relative bodhicitta. Sometimes we take on very big projects that cause us to make a big effort for years, maybe decades or a lifetime. But relative bodhicitta is a project without end, so that when we are successful at one small part of the job, we are happy but don't have unrealistic expectations: tomorrow we will have to start all over again with the business of helping, of righting wrongs, of healing the sick, mending broken hearts.

You may be feeling exhausted just hearing about relative bodhicitta, but actually relative bodhicitta is the antidote to fatigue because it is built on a foundation of absolute bodhicitta. If relative bodhicitta is an endless task, absolute bodhicitta is the endless peace that underlies that endless task. So it's okay. In Zen we frequently chant four vows, the first of which is "Beings are numberless, I vow to save them." What a commitment! Who in their right mind would make such a vow? And yet people who come to Zen centers routinely chant this vow after every lecture, even the first lecture they attend. Maybe they do not notice what they are saying. On one hand, the vow seems like another extravagant and paradoxical Zen expression. Not really. The vow is quite sensible when you think about it: endless need matched perfectly by endless love, endless caring—and this is not something we have to somehow laboriously produce: it is already what we are and how the world works.

Relative bodhicitta: we try hard to help in a practical way, with real feeling.

Absolute bodhicitta: but we don't really need to worry about it, because even if our helping doesn't do any good, it's still okay because of the big love that's everywhere and that heals anyway, no matter what we do, so we can drop the desperate idea that everything is up to us. Everything *is* up to us, but the big us, not the little us, and the big us can take care of it all because it is already taken care of. And because of this, we can love, and we can do our best to help, and we can work really hard, but without having to be burned up by our concern.

So absolute and relative bodhicitta depend on each other as two sides of a coin. Without absolute bodhicitta, relative bodhicitta will become forced and we will become angry and worn out with all of our caring and all of our helping; we can even become furious with the very people we are helping. "Look at all the help I've given you, how come you haven't improved one bit? What's the matter with you? How come you are not grateful? Where is my reward, my prize? At least the smile I was expecting, where's that?" So, helping can become really exhausting and disappointing. That's why we need absolute bodhicitta to sustain us.

And without relative bodhicitta, absolute bodhicitta becomes a kind of grand abstraction, a big, lofty religious idea with no substance to it. What good is a really big love if it never gets applied in the world? What good is a big love if we never love anyone, if we never support anyone? And when we do love someone, when we do support someone, we become awakened, thanks to that person or those people. We become liberated from the dream of self-clinging. We become truly and lastingly happy.

The first slogan for developing absolute bodhicitta (and the second of the fifty-nine slogans) is:

## 2. See everything as a dream.

Everything is always passing away. That's just how it is in this world. As soon as something appears, in that same moment, it's already gone. Everything that exists in time is like this, appearing and disappearing in a flash. That's what we mean when we say "time is passing." Things do certainly seem to be here, I am here, you are here, what you see outside your window is there—but the closer you look, the less clear this is. The me of today must be slightly different from the me of yesterday and the me of tomorrow because I know for certain that the me of fifty years ago is quite different from the me of today, almost completely different. The me of fifty years ago is completely gone, and no trace of him can be found anywhere. He must have disappeared decade by decade, year by year, day by day, and moment by moment. But how? It really doesn't make sense. Now it is today. Where did yesterday go, and where is tomorrow now? You can't say. Nor is it really clear where today—where now—is. As soon as you try to figure it out, it is already gone. Since this is so, you have to wonder whether it was ever really here to begin with, in any hard-and-fast way. Things are always slipping gradually away. If we thought about it even for a moment, we would have to agree. But this is more than a thought. It is also a feeling. If we stop for a moment our busy activity and actually take stock of ourselves as we really are right now, feel our life at this instant, we can note a wistful sense of unease at time passing; we can actually feel this as an underlying mood or sense about life. It is quite unmistakable.

This is what the slogan is pointing out. We actually do live our lives as if in a dream, trying to grab something that isn't really there. Think about this. You are reading this book sometime during a day of your life. Maybe it is early in the morning or late at night. Whatever time of day it is, you assume that the earlier part of the day actually happened, but did it? How can you really verify that? The past is completely gone. And so quickly! There is a memory, yes, a vivid memory, but memory is not the actual concrete fact. It's just memory. Certainly you can find others who will agree with you that today really did happen, and it may never occur to them or you to question it, but what proof do we really have? Mass illusions are certainly possible. Everything is like this—it's a memory—even while it's happening. This is a physiological fact: the brain registers experience a moment after the experience has happened. Life actually, scientifically, is a kind of illusion. It's very hard to actually put your finger on experience. And the closer you look, the stranger it gets. The truth is that there are many things that just don't add up, and you go about your business without investigating. But when you stop to reflect about it, or just stop to look at something or listen to something acutely for a moment or two, just stare at something or try to feel what your own mind feels like—at such moments the oddness of it all comes home to you. Life is like a dream.

You can really appreciate this slogan in meditation practice when you become more present to passing time than you usually are. Here is an experiment you can try, a very simple one: try catching the beginning of any thought or emotion, just as it arises. See if you can grab it right there, just as it first appears in your mind. Sit in meditation, very attentive, very alert, and try to do this. I think you'll discover that this is impossible to do. First there is no thought there, and then somehow, suddenly—as if no time had gone by—you are in the middle of the thought. It didn't have a beginning; it is just there, as if it were there all along. And then it's gone, and you don't know when it started to go, it has just evaporated, without warning. It's really impossible to catch a thought before it arises or to see it pass away. And it's impossible to see your own mind, impossible to see the contents of your mind, because everything is like a dream that appears and disappears, and we don't know where it came from and we don't know where it went.

The important thing about this slogan, the effect it is trying to coax us into, is relief. The same relief that comes when you wake up from that nightmare and your whole body suddenly relaxes because you realize that the dire situation you seemed to be in a moment ago is actually okay, it was just a dream. Your anxiety disappears, and you immediately lighten up and relax. Even the worst things can exude some lightness: "Yes, this is terrible, this is not what I wanted, not what I'd hoped for, not what I'd worked for, maybe even what I had feared. But also it's not that bad. It is like a dream. It's happening and not happening. Soon it will be in the past. So I can look at it differently, I don't need to validate all of these dire thoughts that only make matters worse. Maybe I don't need to be so worked up about it. Maybe I can just figure out how to deal with it without that extra measure of anxiety and freak-out."

This is not a gimmick. Everything really is like a dream. When you train in this slogan, meditate with it, repeat it to yourself, apply it in your daily experience, it begins to change things for you. When you find that you are upset or angry, when you are having a day when you are mad at yourself or someone else and you are hammering on yourself or complaining about someone else for some reason, you can remember to **See everything as a dream,** and your mind will snap into a more alert presence and you will find that you can lighten up to some extent. Everything is passing; every problem, no matter how tough, is already solved, even as it's developing.

The next slogan of absolute bodhicitta is:

## 3. Examine the nature of awareness.

If everything is just a passing memory and you can't really grasp anything, as in a dream, you have to wonder: Who says so? Who knows this? Who is aware of this? Who is reading these words right now?

We know the answer to these questions: "Me! I'm listening to these words. I'm aware of the fact that everything is like a dream, I'm a little skeptical of that, but I'm aware that that's what I just read."

Nothing could be more obvious than this. But have you really examined it? Let me propose another meditation experiment, another experiment in awareness. You could even try it right now. Put the book aside and find yourself, the *me* mentioned in the last paragraph. Find a *yourself,* find a definite, concrete, identifiable *somebody* there within your awareness. . . .

I think you will find this is not so easy to do. You can find plenty of thoughts and emotions, sensations, opinions, sense experiences, but I think it's very difficult to find an *I*. If suddenly, for no reason, your mind were to become very, very quiet and there were only a sound, maybe the sound of silence or the sound of wind or water or machinery, and simply a feeling of presence, and there is nobody complaining and there are no stories going on in your mind, there is only awareness—an experience you may well have in a meditation retreat or maybe any time, in nature, or in spontaneous repose—in that moment there isn't anybody there to congratulate you for it. And as soon as there seems to be someone to notice or congratulate, the experience passes and the inner dialogue resumes. If you should experience a moment like this, it will become instantly clear to you that awareness is something very profound and extremely mysterious and that we really don't know where it comes from or what it is at all. It's powerful, vivid, and very alive, but we don't know what it is. We have a word in our language—*consciousness*—but no one knows what this word means. It's a word that simply covers over our confusion. To recognize this fact and train in it is the burden of this slogan.

Recent brain science corroborates this point. There is, in fact, no brain area, no combination of areas, that corresponds to our sense of "me." Though the sense of "me" does seem to occur subjectively, it is not an experience and does not exist in a location. It emerges somehow from thoughts and emotions that *can* be seen in brain scans, but it itself cannot be seen or measured. It both exists and does not exist at the same time.

The next slogan:

### 4. Don't get stuck on peace.

What **Don't get stuck on peace** means is, more or less, *forget the last two slogans!*

When you practice **See everything as a dream** and **Examine the nature of awareness,** life gets rather dreamy and abstract, as you will have noticed if you have actually been working with them (or even just reading about them). The practice is pleasant but also makes you feel perhaps a bit removed from your life. You begin to focus on the uncanny feeling of time passing, and time begins to seem strange and profound. And it begins to dawn on you that your usual sense of self is some kind of mental habit that might not have any actual basis. You notice how clunky and crude many of your self-thoughts actually are. If all of this is not disturbing to you, and especially if you are a Buddhist or are Buddhist friendly, you might be thinking, "This is great! Everything is empty; everything is a dream, just like the slogan says. There isn't any person in there really, there is just awareness itself, so I'm free of all my self-worries and I can enjoy life a lot more."

What the slogan **Don't get stuck on peace** is saying is that when you start thinking like that, you are caught all over again. You are mistaken. You have merely exchanged one set of confused concepts for another. This train of thought will not be sustainable. It will cause you trouble. The point of **Don't get stuck on peace** is: don't get excited about the empty, dream-like nature of everything, because now you've conceptualized it and made it into something, an idea, and soon that idea is going to trip you up. And forget about how great it is to be nobody, because that's just another excuse. It is too easy to make these slogans into belief systems. The important thing is to hold them lightly and don't think you have understood them. They are just devices. Take them with a grain of salt. They may not really be true at all.

The next slogan offers an alternative:

## 5. Rest in the openness of mind.

The slogan **Rest in the openness of mind** describes a beautiful meditation practice and a beautiful feeling for life. It is a good description of Zen meditation practice, which I always think of as meditation beyond meditation. Not meditating on anything at all or trying to focus the mind or trying to calm the mind or do anything else. Zazen—Zen meditation—is, as one master says, "think not-thinking." It's resting in the openness of mind. Sometimes it's called not knowing. Why would we have to know everything all the time? Why do we have to be so knowledgeable, so smart, so in control? We don't! There's no need to figure everything out. We can just be alive. We can breathe in and breathe out and let go and just trust our life, trust our body. Our body and our life know what to do. The problem is to let them do it, to relax and let them guide us. Of course life is complicated and we have many things to work out in our material and psychological lives. But also we can find a place of refuge sometimes—in our own life, in our own breath, in our own presence. This seems like a very good idea, to have the confidence that that place of refuge exists and that it exists in us. We don't have to search for a powerful guru or a major meditation center or find the best book or method. We can just return right now to ourselves. To our actual concrete presence, in the body, in the breath, in the mind and heart. If we had the confidence that this were possible at any moment, then we would feel much more at ease with our lives and it would be easier and happier to take care of all of our complicated problems. We could do it with far less anxiety and stress. We would trust our life. This slogan points to that trust. Practicing it in meditation or at any time during the day can be quite powerful. **Rest in the openness of mind**. Getting used to this phrase and its meaning so that it can be an inspiration for you, so that you can bring it up at any time during the day, is a powerful advantage.

Maybe the easiest way to do this is also the simplest way: just stop and take a breath. One breath, maybe two or three. You could do this now. Take a breath and return to the openness of mind. Breathing in, breathing out, and in the feeling of the breath noticing whatever is there and letting go of it, easily, gently. Even if you are bored with yourself, even if you have some disturbing things going on in your life that produce disturbing thoughts and feelings in you, it is still possible in this precise moment (even now, as you are reading) to notice breathing, notice the body, notice the feeling of being present in this moment of time. This will relax you. This is what it feels like to **Rest in the openness of mind.**

### 6. In postmeditation be a child of illusion.

Zen practice does not much preserve the distinction most of us would make between meditation and nonmeditation. Zen's emphasis is entirely on presence, on what it really feels like, in this exact moment, to be alive, irrespective of whether we happen to be sitting on our meditation cushion or not. There are many Zen stories whose burden is "Don't be so fixated on meditation as a means of calming the mind and getting insight. Just pay attention to your life right now." These stories are not meant to dissuade us from meditation practice. The word *zen*, after all, does mean meditation. No, the point of these stories is to remind us that spirituality is always about life, not about some particular technique or state of mind. So in Zen there isn't much talk of "meditation and postmeditation."

I lived for many years in Zen monastic and semimonastic communities. My life in those days was pervaded with meditation practice. There were daily meditation and monthly short meditation retreats and, several times a year, weeklong meditation retreats. It was a very disciplined life that involved, as we would say, "following the schedule: the schedule is your teacher." This meant that when it was time for meditation, you went to meditation. And when meditation was over, it was over. You went to work and you did your work in the same spirit. As one Chinese Zen worthy famously put it, "My meditation practice is this: I chop wood, I carry water." He probably meditated too, but when it was time to chop wood, he chopped wood. He didn't have the idea that more meditation was better or that meditation was more important than other things. When it was time to sit, you sat, when time to get up, you got up. Since my wife and I shared child care for our twin sons during a good deal of our Zen training life, which meant that one or the other of us was often doing child care when others were in meditation retreat, this was a very good teaching for us. Meditation is doing what you are doing—whether you are doing formal meditation or child care.

But this slogan is about "postmeditation." It is in contrast to the previous slogan, **Rest in the openness of mind,** which is an instruction for formal meditation. This is what we do on our cushions, as we focus on our body and breathing: we let go of our normal concerns, we relax, we **Rest in the openness of mind.** (Though, as I've said, we can also take a moment to do this at any time.) The present slogan is simply reminding us that the previous slogans, which all point to a sense of life quite different from the ordinary, should be practiced not only on our meditation cushion or moments of repose but also in our ordinary, engaged daily living.

The wording here is important: *be a child of illusion.* Spiritual practice requires a certain degree of childlike innocence. What could be more childlike, if not childish, than to believe that radical spiritual transformation is possible, that the world can be suffused with love, that one can enjoy a measure of happiness and peace in the crazy world we live in? For most people such attitudes, hopes, and beliefs are illusions. They are characteristic of people whose wishful thinking blinds them to the harsh realities. Living with our eyes open, we think, makes us realists who know better than to believe in such pretty fictions. The world is a harsh place. Even the nicest people have their seamy sides; their true motivations are not what they seem. When push comes to shove, everyone is self-interested. And some are even cruel. Only a fool, a child, would think otherwise.

Acknowledging this common and understandable attitude, this slogan encourages us to be childlike, to believe in illusion anyway. This does not mean that we should ignore the other, more difficult, side of life and of humanity, pretend it doesn't exist. Only that we shouldn't let that side completely colonize our minds and hearts. Why not let the innocence that's also there have its place? And who's to say that the world of illusion, the world of the child, is less real than the brutally realistic world of the adult? Do we believe that, that children are foolish? That the world they live in is an illusion? Of course not. A child's world is real, as real as any other. Children cheer us up. Life can be gruesome, many very tough things can be going on, but when you see a child, if you can suspend for a moment your grim preoccupation and take in the child's reality, you are instantly cheered, at least for a moment, because there is something endearing and strongly positive in a child's world—a world we have all inhabited and been formed by but have abandoned. Yet that world still exists in us too. Why not cultivate it, recall it, in our everyday lives? Why not have, along with our appropriate adult perspective, a child's-eye view of the world? After all, we have been practicing seeing everything as a dream, examining unborn awareness, and resting in the openness of mind. This slogan tells us to take these practices into our everyday lives, postmeditation, and introduce an element of childlike delight. Maybe we can cheer ourselves up.

There are many ways to practice this. You can stop every now and then and look out the window. What do you see out there: a tree, the sky, a tall building? Whatever it is, why not take it in for a moment with wonder. What about the person in your life who has been giving you a hard time these days? Why not call her to mind or, even now, as you are talking to her and looking at her, notice her eyes and ears and nose and marvel at them. Defamiliarize yourself for a moment, let your usual mind-set go, and be amazed by what is immediately there in front of you. You can cultivate the habit of being a child of illusion now and then, or unhooking yourself from conventional reality. Because conventional reality is not the only reality. It is a reality, an important reality, and one we have to deal with. But it is not the only reality, and thinking it is only hems us in, imprisons and confines us, which makes living in conventional reality that much more difficult. When we practice being children of illusion, we expand and loosen our grip on conventional reality. This may not only ease our feeling of burden—it may also help us to find solutions to problems in conventional reality we might not otherwise have seen.

So these are the five slogans of absolute bodhicitta. Practicing them expands and smoothes the space we are living in, breaking down the walls we've been putting up for so long, maybe without realizing it, walls that have been causing us so much pain and sorrow and loneliness. These walls have also been causing pain to others. Each one of us could be a source of joy for ourselves and for everyone who knows us. Maybe you know someone who is like this, and whenever you are with this person you feel happy. A person like this is a blessing for the world. And there is no reason why you couldn't be that person. Why aren't you that person now? Because of these walls of self-protection you've built, these attitudes of limit and lack. Practicing these slogans and reflecting on the meaning of absolute bodhicitta, you can allow those walls and those attitudes to fall down. Resting childlike in openness of mind in this dream-like life, you will feel protected and at peace. You will feel not only that you are loved but that love is built into the nature of what you are and of what the world is, so that you are never apart from it. Knowing this, you can risk caring and loving. You don't have to be afraid of it anymore. You will not be hurt. Your love will be received, and it will always be healing. Knowing this is so through the practice of these slogans, you can begin to practice relative bodhicitta.

# 3

## Train in Empathy and Compassion

PART 2: *Relative Compassion*

WE HAVE JUST CONTEMPLATED the slogans that teach absolute bodhicitta, the reality that life is essentially dream-like and built on a foundation of love. It should be obvious, but is perhaps worth noting, that the slogans don't assume that at this point you will have perfect insight into these profound realities. The intention and the hope is, rather, that contemplating the slogans will give you a respectful appreciation for these truths and the beginnings of some faith in them. And that this will be sufficient for you to progress to the second part of the **Training in empathy and compassion,** the more hands-on, more easily understood, but perhaps more difficult part, relative bodhicitta.

Relative bodhicitta is difficult because loving actual people as they really are, in this imperfect world as it really is, always involves some pain. Obviously it won't do to love somebody and enjoy that person's company but then, when things between you get difficult, to abandon the person. No, it is clear that as pleasant as love is, it must also be unpleasant, because people are sometimes unpleasant or go through unpleasant things, and if we abandon them at those times and run away from them because they or their situation has become unpleasant, we would have to conclude that there wasn't much to our loving in the first place. It would make no sense at all, for instance, if we love someone, to say to that person, "Well, now you are getting a little difficult and I am not enjoying you today, so I guess our association should end." Or "Now you are having a hard time in your life or you are ill or now you are dying, and I find this not so inspiring, not so nice to be around, and because of this it's getting a little hard for me to love you, so I guess I'll find someone who is not difficult, not ill, not dying, to love and forget about you, because this is not so nice for me. Sorry about that, but I hope you understand." If someone were to say such things to us in such circumstances, I am sure we would *not* understand and would feel terribly wounded and betrayed and would not think that this was a speech given to us by someone who ever really loved us at all. Beyond being abandoned now, we would be dismayed at the thought that the love we thought we had enjoyed had never been anything more than a horrible charade.

Of course, exactly such speeches (more or less) are recited every day, because for many people love is too difficult to sustain exactly because it requires that we have the capacity to accept painful situations. Even under the best of circumstances, pain will eventually come as a consequence of love, because it's guaranteed that we will lose the beloved. Not sometimes, not often, but 100 percent of the time the one that we love will leave us or we will leave him or her, through death, in the end, if not in some other way. All relationships end in parting and loss—romantic relationships and all other associations of caring.

I often say to people, "If you want to understand suffering, there is one sure way to do it—love!" The reverse is also true: if you want to understand love, you are going to have to understand suffering. This is why the practice of this relative bodhicitta is as difficult as it is wonderful.

The original *Seven Points of Training the Mind* text is famous for introducing a meditation practice called sending and receiving (*tonglen*).

Every form of religion, and every form of Buddhism, has its cultural prejudices, and in Zen practice (especially my school of Zen, Soto Zen), the prejudice is to be antitechnique. As I've said, Zen even denies the difference between meditation and nonmeditation. How much more, then, would it be resistant to particular meditation techniques? Zen meditation is radically simple: just sit still and breathe and see what happens. Everything else seems overly fancy. So in Zen if we practice special techniques, we always hold them very lightly, without worrying too much about the details or taking them too seriously. Focusing on technique as technique seems somehow against the whole proposition of religion. It just doesn't seem reasonable that our spiritual well-being is somehow going to be ensured if we master a technique, that religion is an art form, a matter of virtuosity. Or that the reverse would be so, that somehow our spiritual path would be wrecked or invalidated because we can't master a certain technique. On the other hand, it would also be foolish to have a dogmatic principle against any technique. Sometimes a technique can come in handy when you need it. So, given this antitechnique prejudice and this flexible spirit of willing curiosity, we take up the technique of sending and receiving.

There are two slogans that describe the practice:

7. **Practice sending and receiving alternately on the breath.**
8. **Begin sending and receiving practice with yourself.**

Sending and receiving is a technique to directly develop compassion. Remember that *compassion* literally means "to feel passion with." Passion means pain. Compassion is the willingness to feel pain with another, to feel another's pain as one's own. We usually think of compassion as something sweet and nice, positive and wonderful. Everybody wants to be compassionate. And it's true—compassion feels good. But we overlook the fact that compassion is also essentially a painful feeling. Feeling another's pain as our own is painful. And it turns out that it's impossible to take in the pain of another unless we are able to take in our own pain. And most of us are not so good at accepting our own pain; we prefer to deny it or distract ourselves from it. We are so intent on making our own pain go away that we don't allow ourselves to feel it. We can't take it in. Consequently we are incapable of feeling another's pain, so we are incapable of actual compassion, although we may think we are quite compassionate.

If you've ever been ill, physically or emotionally, or otherwise in need of compassionate caring, you may have noticed that many people will offer help and kind words, but somehow most of these offerings seem either insincere or otherwise to miss the mark. They don't feel good, they don't help. It is as if these people, though they clearly mean well and their offers are touching, are not capable of really receiving your pain. They want to make you feel better, help you somehow by offering remedies and recommendations or cheerful words or distracting gifts, but they seem unable or unwilling to do what you need them to do: to simply feel and acknowledge your pain. They want to be compassionate, but they can't seem to do that, and so their presence makes you feel more lonely and isolated in your misfortune. This is because they are actually terrified of their own pain. And you can feel that they are also terrified of your pain, even though, of course, they would never say so and may not even realize they are feeling this. But you, the person ill in a hospital bed or depressed or grieving, can see this all too clearly. And when you are in need of compassion, these people do not really comfort you. Maybe they even annoy you, despite their sincere efforts. Because it is impossible to be truly compassionate, to receive another's pain, if you are unable to receive your own.

This reminds me of the time of my mother's death, decades ago. She was a dear woman, but very bewildered by what was happening to her, and quite agitated. She was only sixty-two, never expected to die so young, and didn't really know she was dying now. Or maybe she did know but couldn't bear to think about it, and no one around her ever brought it up. We were all there, me, my brother, my father, and my mother's sisters. Probably what my mother needed, in her agitated state, was a little peace and quiet. But instead she was constantly interrupted by nurses and doctors looking in on her and by relatives who kept turning her pillow, asking her what she needed, getting her things she didn't need, and trying to talk to her about cheerful things. But it seemed obvious to me that none of us could accept the reality of my mother's situation, because none of us had made peace with the fact that this was death, that she would die, we would die, and that we all felt terrible about this situation. None of us could face the pain—ours or hers.

Another dear friend of mine lost her husband, who died suddenly, with no warning. His death was a complete shock to her, and her subsequent grief was so immense that she was all but inconsolable. She had many friends who kept trying to comfort her. Not only did their efforts leave her completely untouched, they actually made her angry. Her grief had given her a deadly accurate insincerity meter, so she felt people's fear and avoidance much more than she felt the consolation they were trying to offer her with their words and pats on the shoulder. This, I think, is common in grief. You can tell quite easily who is and who is not really willing and able to go where you are, in your deep sorrow, and you can be quite upset by the pious conventional words and gestures of those who want to be nice and compassionate but actually have no clue as to what compassion actually is. Compassion really does require us to feel the pain of another personally.

The practice of sending and receiving has two main purposes: first, to train your heart to do what it usually does not want to do: to go toward, rather than away from, what's painful and difficult in your own life; and second, to realize that your own suffering and the suffering of others are not different. When you discover that this is so, you see that when you are willing to really take in your own suffering, you find, within that very suffering, the suffering of others; and the reverse is also true: when you are able to truly take in the suffering of another, you find within it your own human pain. Being willing to receive pain, we come to understand, is the only way to open our hearts to love. The practice will make this an experiential truth.

Sending and receiving begins and ends with the absolute bodhicitta slogan **Rest in the openness of mind**. It is this comforting and supportive resting that gives us the basis we need for the hard work that the practice entails. In the beginning we gather courage from it, and in the end we return to it for rest and recuperation.

Start by breathing in the openness of mind that you can feel in the clarity and strength of the inhale. And then exhale, letting go completely and merging with openness of mind, so that there is nothing else present but that. Breathing this way, we open to a complete release of everything and trust of everything, especially when we exhale, resting in the natural openness of our own being and of everything. In a way, there is nothing at all to this. It's no big deal. It's not colorful, it's not spectacular, it's not profound or special. It's just an easeful opening and letting go. It feels as if we're floating, buoyed up by the waters of reality. That's how we begin the practice, staying with this part for as long as we need to.

Next, we practice sending and receiving, as the slogan says: practice them alternately; they should ride the breath. So the next time we breathe in, we breathe in our own pain and the suffering. Not only do we not avoid it as we usually do, as it is our natural impulse to do, we actually breathe it into our body. We gobble up all the suffering and the pain. We may well be squeamish about this, and it might be difficult at first, but with practice we can do it. We can visualize the pain and suffering as a dark, sticky substance or smoke or some kind of goo that we are breathing in, taking into our bodies. The goo is coming from all around us, and we are taking it in, with all the pores of our body as well as though our nostrils as we breathe in. If you are not so visually oriented and this image of goo is not useful, then in some other way imagine that you are actually breathing in the pain and suffering, really taking it in. This is receiving.

Of course, we don't only breathe in, we also breathe out. When we breathe out, something miraculous happens. It turns out that our bodies are transformation machines. They transform the goo, the suffering, the pain, into lightness, ease, peacefulness that comes out of our nostrils and all the pores of our body as a light sweet mist (or if you are not visually oriented, as a more imaginative and vague sense of lightness and ease, maybe even joy). Unharmed by the pain we breathed in, we have now transformed that pain, so that we now breathe out bliss and ease and lightness and healing power, as if we were breathing out healing light. This is sending. We are sending healing light to ourselves and to many others.

The reason it works this way is that absolute bodhicitta is the nature of our human body. Our body has a wisdom greater than we ever imagined. After all, it breathes, it circulates blood, it heals us, keeps us balanced and alive every day, without our paying attention to it. It has been miraculously born into this world, through no effort on our part, and when it is finished doing its work, at that precise moment, without fanfare and without regret, it lets go of life and returns to the earth it is made of. (We may have many regrets and clingings, but the body doesn't; it knows exactly what to do.) Our life, in fact, is a sacred miracle. We constantly forget this, occupied as we are with other matters. But fortunately our body never forgets. Our body never fails us, for it is, on its own, as it is, love itself. It is life itself, nature itself, flowing on in profound sanity and appreciation despite our human confusion. Naturally it has the capacity to breathe in suffering and transform it into healing. In fact, this is what breathing is: breathing in we are saying yes to another moment of life with all of its pain, sorrow, and loss; breathing out we are releasing all of this, we are letting go of everything in this moment, returning to peace. I do not think I am elaborating or exaggerating when I describe the physiological process of breathing in this poetic way. To me it is not poetic. It is simply true. Why would we think this explanation less true than the other explanation we have, which is also useful to us, that the blood is oxygenated by the breath and so on. We need to appreciate both explanations.

So when we are willing, intentionally, with this kind of attitude, this vision, to breathe in the suffering, we are able to transform it easily and naturally; it doesn't take a major effort on our part, other than that we allow it. So that now, when we breathe out, it's not suffering anymore, we are not breathing out suffering, we are breathing out easeful healing light, because the suffering has turned into that healing light. And that's the practice of sending, sending out that healing energy to the world.

As the slogan says, this process starts with yourself. You begin by breathing in your own pain and suffering. Whether it's your anger or your fear, your confusion, your grief, your loss, your resentment, your disappointment, maybe your hatred of some person, whatever it is, you breathe it in. Or maybe you have an illness. Then you breathe in your illness, your cancer, your pain, your weak or damaged heart, your confused immune system. You breathe in the poison of your illness, and you fully digest it and you send out healing and blissful energy to yourself, you send it back to yourself.

After you practice with yourself for a while, it becomes natural to practice with another, with someone you know well and care about. You will want to do this. Maybe the person is ill or in some sort of trouble. This is someone you really care about and would like to help, and now you can: you breathe in the person's suffering. You take it from him or her into your body with the breath. And thanks to the spiritual power inherent in your body, you can do this without being harmed, and now you can breathe out the suffering as peaceful, healing, soothing relief. It's not suffering anymore; the suffering has been transformed.

And then, after you've practiced that way for a while, you can breathe in all of the suffering, all the suffering of the world, the whole mass of suffering of everyone and everything, the plants, the animals, the sea and sky—you breathe it all in—and you breathe out a long, slow, gentle breath of healing and relief for the world and all that's in it.

After practicing this way for a while, you return to the beginning, to the openness of mind, letting go of all of the suffering and all of the relief and just resting again in the simple openness of mind.

Sending and receiving practice might seem daunting when you first hear about it. It might seem impossible. But keep in mind that the point is not to be able to do all of this perfectly, exactly as described, but simply to try your best to do whatever you can. When you try the practice, you will probably notice a strong resistance to the first step: breathing in your own suffering. You might find this nearly impossible to do. And it might bring up fear, anger, resentment, even terror. If so, relax and return to openness of mind. You can try again later. It's important to take the practice slowly and gently and to pay attention to fear and resistance for what it is, to realize that feeling these things is not a barrier to the practice—it *is* the practice at this stage. Your fear and resistance are your path right now, so it is important not to back away from them but to engage them.

If breathing in your own suffering is this difficult, it might seem completely impossible to breathe in the suffering of the whole world. But sometimes it is easier to breath in the suffering of others and even the whole world than to breathe in our own pain. The best way is to go on with the stages of the practice as best you can and just see, with honesty and without jumping to the usual conclusions, what happens. Whatever thought or emotion is present in you at any moment in the practice needs to be there, whether you like it or not and whether it accords with the instructions or not. If it didn't need to be there, why would it be there? Was there some sort of slipup in reality? Does reality have slipups? No; whatever is here is what's here, it's what we have to work with. Self-judgment or second-guessing or doubt is useless. But if self-judgment or second-guessing or doubt is what is here, then we practice with it. So if you decide to do this practice and you feel resistance—you even hate it—at any point in the practice, this is all part of the practice: you breathe in the hatred and resistance and fear as a sticky, gooey substance, and you breathe out relief, healing, lightness, ease. In this way there are no excuses and no barriers. Whatever is going on, no matter how seemingly counterproductive, can be received, transformed, and sent back out as positive energy.

Sending and receiving is something I practice regularly. I've described here a version of a traditional practice, but it can also be done more simply, with the basic idea of breathing in suffering and breathing out relief. It can be practiced informally, off the meditation cushion, in a moment of meeting someone who is suffering or in a moment of feeling your own suffering when something difficult suddenly happens (something large or small, even a minor irritation: it is a feature of this practice, and of Buddhist practice in general, that small things and large things are both important and to be taken seriously—and lightly). In this way sending and receiving can be quite a serviceable way of training ourselves to relax or even entirely overcome our reflexive habit of turning away from what's difficult, thereby most of the time compounding the difficulty.

Earlier I mentioned my mother's dying. I wish I had known sending and receiving practice then. I have since then practiced it many times for my mother, and I practice it regularly for my friends who are ill or dying or have died. It is enormously helpful to me to no longer feel powerless or at a loss during these difficult times and instead to have a practice that keeps the person constantly on my mind in a way that helps me to feel connected to his or her suffering without feeling enmeshed or capsized by it. Practicing sending and receiving for my friends over the years has increased both my sadness and my joy—and made my heart much more tender toward everyone I meet.

The next slogan of relative bodhicitta:

### 9. Turn things around.

My restatement of the traditional form of this slogan—Three objects, three poisons, three seeds of virtue—is simple: **Turn things around**. Where there's confusion or pain in your life, make use of it instead of trying to get rid of it. Trying to get rid of it usually doesn't work anyway. It only makes things worse. (Of course, if your painful situation can be resolved somehow, resolve it. The practice is not encouraging us to accept bad situations that can be improved; it is addressing the pesky facts and emotional states that are not so simply removed: grief, fear, and so on.)

To discuss how this works, I will refer to the traditional statement of the slogan, "Three objects, three poisons, three seeds of virtue." This Buddhist language requires some explanation. *Three objects* refers to three categories of objects. According to Buddhist thought, every object falls into one of these three categories. And *object*, interestingly, doesn't refer merely to physical objects. Thoughts and feelings are also "objects," objects of consciousness, just as all so-called physical objects are objects of perception. Early Buddhist thought, which is almost entirely concerned with liberation for the human mind and heart rather than with dispassionate investigation of truth, is remarkable in its anticipation of many of the insights of contemporary cognitive science. In this case, what's being highlighted is the fact that in terms of human life and experience, the world "out there" is really the world "in here," that is, the world of our perception, feeling, and thought. "Green" is not a substance that inheres in an object: it is an experience that takes place in our brain when it is stimulated by an object bathed in light. And similarly, our mind may have as its "object" the inner feeling of anger or love, which arises in response to outer or inner events or objects.

The three categories into which all objects fall are attractive, unattractive, and neutral. That is, the objects themselves do not have these qualities but our reactions to the objects do. Buddhist psychology posits that our minds cannot be objective. Even perception is not objective. Whatever comes into our consciousness will spur a reaction in us, and this reaction will be, in its simplest form, one of these three: we will either like, dislike, or be neutral to the object (or have both like and dislike, which amounts to neutrality).

This is what is meant by the phrase "three objects": three sorts of reactions that, for our experience, seem attached to all objects. The "three poisons" (greed, hate, and delusion) are the emotional activities we indulge in in response to the three objects. We are greedy for objects we like (*greed* here meaning, basically, we want to go toward the attractive object), aversive to objects we don't like (hatred), and confused or indifferent about objects to which we are neutral (delusion).

The three objects and three poisons describe basic ordinary daily life. "Objects" constantly arise, and we are constantly trying to grab them and make them stay or push them away as soon as possible, depending on the style of our reactivity and emotion. The flow of these objects and emotions goes on constantly, usually below the level of conscious awareness. We wake up in the morning and feel too cold or too hot or just right. This makes us feel pleasant or irritated or neutral. Our coffee is tasty or not so tasty, and we're slightly pleased or annoyed. Our thoughts are pleasant or not so pleasant. All day long objects appear to our perception, feeling, and thought, and all day long we are reacting in simple, basic ways to each and every object: wonderful, let's keep this one; terrible, let's get rid of this one; neutral, I don't care about this one.

All day long this flows on, usually without much discernable problem. But occasionally our likes or dislikes become strongly activated by objects, and then we become powerfully happy or miserable, overcome with lust or desire or anger or fear.

All day long, based on this flow of experience, we are making tiny and sometimes large choices. We never choose the things we don't like; we choose the things we like. To some extent, we have control over our choices—unfortunately, ultimately, and sadly for us, not enough control. Quite often we cannot avoid losing what we find attractive and having to put up with what we find unattractive. And in the biggest picture of our lives, we always end up losing what we want (our loved ones, our health) and having to put up with what we don't want (our aging, our illness, our death, and the loss of our loved ones). Our efforts to control the world to suit ourselves will ultimately be unsuccessful, and if we insist on trying desperately to control things we can't control, we eventually become very desperate and unhappy; the world begins to seem like a very hostile and unjust place, and we can become quite paranoid and upset about almost everything. Because once you decide that the world is a hostile and inhospitable place and the people in it untrustworthy and venal, things begin to get worse and worse and worse. So the three objects and three poisons are lamentable realities. If we don't pay attention to them, if we don't figure out a way to cooperate with rather than resist their pressure, they can ruin our lives.

Against this background, the slogan is startling. It's saying that contrary to what we might think, the three objects and three poisons are not problems and traps; they are three seeds of goodness, three seeds of virtue. In other words, the basic human mess of likes and dislikes, in which we seem to be trapped and which seems to be so dangerous and troublesome, is actually wonderful, a real treasure. Our messes and our problems are our treasures! Zen master Shunryu Suzuki wrote, "For Zen students, a weed is a treasure." Our suffering, our troubles, our problems, the things that we really don't like and want to get rid of but can't, or the losses we feel, the things we wanted to keep and sadly cannot—all of this is a treasure to us if only we can understand it in the right way. Everything painful and difficult has the potential to bring us great joy and deep spiritual riches.

Knowing this, we can **Turn things around**. We can turn toward and appreciate our suffering, our problems, and the suffering and problems of others. This is the ultimate position for our spiritual path. Given the power of our likes and dislikes and the intractability of the world (which doesn't necessarily organize itself according to our needs), it won't do not to deal with our likes and dislikes in some way other than simply trying constantly to fulfill them. So naturally we imagine somehow trying to modify or eliminate them. This slogan is saying something radically different: it's through our very likes and dislikes and the suffering they bring us that we can find spiritual growth.

We can practice this slogan by writing it down, contemplating it carefully, and bringing it up when we find ourselves annoyed or upset by instances of liking and disliking that are causing us suffering. This practice might help us to let go a little in that moment. Even if we don't believe it and are, at this point, only a little intrigued by it, it can be helpful to practice this slogan. It will have the effect of causing us to stop our lamentation for a moment and recall that it might just be possible that there is something potentially good and positive in this agony we are right now enmeshed in.

It is easy to see how this slogan fits with the practice of sending and receiving. That practice trains us to see and feel that our pain and difficulty in this life, and the pain and the difficulty of others, is the gateway that will lead us down the path of love. We don't need to avoid or protect ourselves from pain. Quite the contrary. When pain and suffering are present, we need to turn toward them, breathe them in. And through this practice of accepting suffering we can transform it—and transform ourselves in the bargain.

What a difference this would make in your life if you actually knew that when things happen that you don't like, that are difficult or painful, you don't need to complain and try fruitlessly to change them (when they can't be changed), and that you don't need to find someone to blame and then do battle with that blameworthy person, as if you were a victim, but instead you can have a profound and heartfelt sense of acceptance and love, you can breathe in the difficulty and transform it into ease and healing through your body. Suppose you understood all of your pain and suffering as raw material for transformation and healing. Your life would be completely different.

These relative bodhicitta slogans are deep and difficult. They re-quire cultivation over time, persistence, diligence, and strength. As if in acknowledgement of this, the last slogan in this section is a simple one that requires no explanation. It reminds us to keep on with our effort all of the time, in everything we do:

**10. Always train with the slogans.**

# 4

## Transform Bad Circumstances into the Path

THERE'S AN OLD ZEN SAYING: *the whole world's upside down.* In other words, the way the world looks from the ordinary or conventional point of view is pretty much the opposite of the way the world actually is (at least as far as the Zen masters have conceived of it). There's a story that illustrates this. Once there was a Zen master called Bird's Nest Roshi because he meditated in an eagle's nest at the top of a tree. This was quite a dangerous thing to do: one gust of wind, one sleepy moment, and he was done for. He became quite famous for this precarious practice. The Song Dynasty poet Su Shih (who was also a government official) once came to visit him and, standing on the ground far below the meditating master, asked what possessed him to live in such a dangerous manner. The roshi answered, "You call this dangerous? What you are doing is far more dangerous!" Living normally in the world, ignoring death, impermanence, and loss and suffering, as we all routinely do, as if this were a normal and a safe way to live, is actually much more dangerous than going out on a limb to meditate.

As we have been saying, while trying to avoid difficulty may be natural and understandable, it actually doesn't work. We think it makes sense to protect ourselves from pain, but our self-protection ends up causing us deeper pain. We think we have to hold on to what we have, but our very holding on causes us to lose what we have. We're attached to what we like and try to avoid what we don't like, but we can't keep the attractive object and we can't avoid the unwanted object. So, counterintuitive though it may be, avoiding life's difficulties is actually not the path of least resistance: it is a dangerous way to live. If you want to have a full and happy life, in good times and bad, you have to get used to the idea that facing misfortune squarely is better than trying to escape from it.

This is not a matter of grimly focusing on life's difficulties. It is simply the smoothest possible approach to happiness. As we have already learned through the practice of sending and receiving, being willing to breathe in difficulty and transform it into healing, and even joy, is much better than fruitlessly trying to escape from it. Of course, when we can prevent difficulty, we do that. The world may be upside down, but we still have to live in this upside-down world, we have to be practical on its terms. So yes, we do reasonably try to protect our investments, get regular checkups, exercise, take care of our diet, get homeowner's insurance, and so on. Point three doesn't deny any of that. Instead, it addresses the underlying attitude of anxiety, fear, and narrow-mindedness that makes our lives unhappy, fearful, and small.

The practice of **Transforming bad circumstances into the path** is associated with the practice of patience, my all-time favorite spiritual quality. Patience is the capacity to welcome difficulty when it comes, with a spirit of strength, endurance, forbearance, and dignity rather than fear, anxiety, and avoidance. None of us likes to be oppressed or defeated, yet if we can endure oppression and defeat with strength, without whining, we are ennobled by it. Patience makes this possible. Still, in our culture, we think of patience as passive and unglamorous. Other qualities like love or compassion or insight are much more popular. Naturally, we want the good stuff, the pleasant and inspiring stuff. But when tough times cause our love to fray into annoyance, our compassion to be overwhelmed by our fear, and our insight to evaporate, then patience begins to make sense. To me it is the most substantial, most serviceable, and most reliable of all spiritual qualities. Without it all other qualities are shaky.

The practice of patience is simple enough. When difficulty arises, notice the obvious and not so obvious ways we try to avoid it. The things we say and do, the subtle ways in which our very bodies recoil and clench when someone says or does something to us that we don't like. To practice patience is to simply notice these things and be fiercely present with them (taking a breath helps; returning to mindfulness of the body helps) rather than reacting to them and flailing around. Paying attention to body, paying attention to mind. And when possible, giving ourselves good teachings about the virtue of being with, rather than trying to run away from, the anguish we are feeling in this moment.

There are six slogans under this third point:

11. **Turn all mishaps into the path.**
12. **Drive all blames into one.**
13. **Be grateful to everyone.**
14. **See confusion as Buddha and practice emptiness.**
15. **Do good, avoid evil, appreciate your lunacy, pray for help.**
16. **Whatever you meet is the path.**

The first slogan, **Turn all mishaps into the path,** sounds at first blush completely impossible. How would you do that? When things go all right we are cheerful, we feel good and have good spiritual feelings, but as soon as bad things start happening, we get depressed, we fall apart, or at the very best, we hang on and cope. We certainly do not transform our mishaps into the path. And why would we want to? We don't want the mishaps to be there, we want them gone as soon as possible. They are certainly not the path! The path is love and light, compassion, joy, and so on, we think.

But keep in mind that **Transform bad circumstances into the path** is the third point of mind training. It comes after the first slogan, **Train in the preliminaries,** which one presumably has done thoroughly, and after the practices of generating compassion, as we've discussed. Having established all of that, we have shaken up our conventional point of view. We are beginning to be more like the Bird's Nest Roshi than the poet below him, beginning to recognize that perhaps our habitual ways of thinking about our lives need to be reexamined. Also, we have been training in the practice of slogans, repeating them over and over, reflecting on them repeatedly, so that now they often pop up naturally, unbidden, when we need them. Now when something difficult or terrible happens to us, a loss, a setback, a frustration, an insult, naturally we immediately feel dismay or anger or disappointment or resentment just as everyone does, just as we always have—but now also a slogan pops into our minds, because we have trained ourselves in it. *Turn all of this into the path,* the slogan tells us.

So we practice patience: we catch ourselves running away and we reverse course, turning toward our afflictive emotions, understanding that they are natural in these circumstances but that avoiding them won't work and that there is no use blaming ourselves or wishing that things were otherwise. We know that this is how the human heart works, this is how we all are. We forestall our flailing around with these emotions and instead allow them to be present with dignity. We forgive ourselves for having them, we forgive whoever we might be blaming for our difficulties, and with that spontaneous forgiveness comes a feeling of relief and even gratitude. We think: "Oh, yes, I really am angry right now, I am pretty upset right now, but this doesn't belong to me, this upset is what people feel under such conditions, and of course I feel this way. And I am grateful to feel what everyone feels under such conditions. I am glad to stand in solidarity and understanding with other human beings who are probably, right now, in this very moment, also feeling this."

This may strike you as a bit far-fetched, but it is not. Yet it does take training: we are, after all, not talking about miracles, we are not talking about affirmations or wishful thinking. We are talking about training the mind. If you were to meditate daily, bringing up this slogan, **Turn all mishaps into the path,** in your sitting, writing it down, repeating it many times a day, reflecting on it, reading the words of this book many times and thinking about them, then you could see that a change of heart and mind could take place in just the way I am describing. It simply makes sense. The mind and heart react according to their well-worn habits. Whatever habit of mind you have now comes from your actions and thoughts of the past (however unexamined or unintentional they may have been). Whatever habits of mind you will have in future depend on what you do or don't do from now on. The way you spontaneously react in times of trouble is not fixed. Your mind, your heart, can be trained. Once you have a single experience of reacting differently, you will be encouraged. Next time it is more likely that you will take yourself in hand. Each time becomes easier than the last. And little by little you establish a new habit. When something difficult happens, you will train yourself to stop saying, "Damn! Why did this have to happen!" and begin saying, "Yes, of course, this is how it is, let me turn toward it, let me practice with it, let me go beyond entanglement to gratitude." Because you will have realized that because you are alive and not dead, because you have a human body and not some other kind of a body, because the world is a physical world and not an ethereal world, and because all of us together as people are the way we are, bad things are going to happen. It's the most natural, the most normal, the most inevitable thing in the world. It is not a mistake, and it isn't anyone's fault. And we can make use of it to drive our gratitude and our compassion deeper.

The second slogan under this third point of training the heart is famous: **Drive all blames into one.** It, too, is quite counterintuitive, quite upside down. What it is saying is: whatever happens, don't ever blame anyone or anything else, always blame only yourself. Eat the blame and it will make you strong.

There's another Zen story about this one. In Zen there's a formal eating ritual called *oryoki*. In Zen monasteries this is the way the monks eat all of their meals: in robes, seated on meditation cushions on raised platforms, with formal serving and chanting, eating in a dignified prescribed style, even washing out the bowls with water and wiping and putting them away as part of the ritual. When I was a monastic, I ate this way every day, and even now at some of our retreats we practice oryoki. At first the practice seems intimidating and overly complicated, but when you do it for a while, it becomes second nature and you see its beauty. You realize that actually it is the simplest, most elegant, and most efficient way that a group of people could eat together. In a way, it is a bit like mind training itself: it seems at first impossible and complicated, but when you get used to it, you see how beautiful and even how simple and natural it is.

In any case, once in ancient China an abbot was eating oryoki style with the monks in the meditation hall. He discovered a snake head in his soup. This was not snake soup; Zen monasteries are vegetarian. It was definitely a mistake. Probably a farmer monk out in the fields hadn't noticed that he'd cut off the head of a snake while cutting the greens, and the snake's head had found its way into the soup pot because the soup-cook monk also hadn't noticed it. Such things happen, even when you are practicing mindfulness and doing good organic farming and trying not to kill anything. But a mistake is a mistake, and a mistake that ends up in the abbot's bowl is a mistake compounded. The abbot called the *tenzo,* the head cook. "Look!" He held up the snake's head. And the tenzo, without saying a word, snatched the snake's head and swallowed it. He didn't blame the farmer, he didn't blame the soup cook. He didn't make excuses. He didn't feel guilty or ashamed. He ate the blame. It was probably very nourishing.

**Drive all blames into one** is tricky because blaming ourselves, which seems to be what the slogan is recommending, is not exactly blaming ourselves in the ordinary sense. We know perfectly well how to blame ourselves. We've been doing this all of our lives, it is commonplace; we are constantly feeling guilty about everything, and if we are not guilty, we are ashamed. We don't need Buddhist slogans to tell us to do this. But clearly this is not what is meant.

**Drive all blames into one** means that you can't blame anyone for what happens, even if it's actually someone's fault, like the farmer's or the soup cook's. It may be their fault, but you really can't blame them. Something happened, and since it did, there is nothing else to be done but to make use of it. Everything that happens, disastrous as it may be, and no matter whose fault it is, has a potential benefit, no matter how bad it may seem at first. That's the nature of something happening, that it has a potential benefit, and it's your job to find out how to turn it into a benefit. **Drive all blames into one** means that you take the full appreciation and full responsibility for everything that arises in your life, no matter whose fault it is. This is very bad, this is not what I wanted, this brings many attendant problems. But what are you going to do with it? What can you learn from it? How can you make use of it for the path? These are the questions to ask, and answering them is entirely up to you. Furthermore, you *can* answer them; you do have the strength and the capacity. **Drive all blames into one** is a tremendous practice of cutting through the long human habit of complaining and whining, and finding on the other side of all of that the strength to turn every situation into the path.

Blaming others and blaming yourself are actually not so different when you examine them. How is it possible to blame yourself? The only way is to stand next to yourself wagging your finger at yourself, just the way you wag your finger at someone else you are blaming for something. Blaming yourself requires that you somehow stand outside yourself and scrutinize yourself, removing yourself from yourself so as to make yourself into somebody else that you could blame. This seems absurd, but when you examine it, this is exactly what happens. There is no way to be self-blaming or self- incriminating without self-externalizing. Self-judging is self-externalizing. But the question is, who is it that is standing over there wagging her or his finger at whom? So it doesn't matter whom you blame—self or another, it is more or less the same thing. The important point is to accept that what has happened has actually happened. Without hesitation you eat the snake head. You accept reality, you accept responsibility, and you figure out what to do next. And if you can't shake the recriminations? You breathe them in, you breathe them out, you try your best to stay present and patient and not let your mind run away with you. Here you are. This is it. It is not some other way, it is this way. There is no place else to go but forward into the next moment. Repeat the slogan as many times as you have to.

The third slogan under point three is: **Be grateful to everyone.** Very simple but very profound.

My wife and I have a grandson. We went to visit him when he was about six weeks old. He couldn't do anything, not even hold up his head, much less feed himself. If he was in trouble, he couldn't ask for help. If suddenly he found his hand in his mouth and he began chewing on his hand, he didn't know what that was or who it belonged to. And if he liked the hand in his mouth and it fell out of his mouth, he couldn't figure out how to get it back in. He had no idea of anything in the world. He had his likes and dislikes, certainly, but he was powerless to do anything but experience them as the world changed every moment, not necessarily to his advantage. Unable to do anything on his own, he was completely dependent on his mother's care and constant attention. She fed him, cuddled him, tried to understand and anticipate his needs, took care of everything, including his peeing and pooping.

We were all at one time precisely in this situation, and someone or other must have cared for us in this same comprehensive way. Without 100 percent total care from someone else, or maybe several others, we would not be here. This is certainly grounds for gratitude to others.

But our dependence on others did not end there. We didn't grow up and become independent. Now we can hold up our heads, fix our dinner, wipe our butt, and we seem not to need our mother or father to take care us—so we think we are autonomous. We think there is no longer a need to be grateful to others for our lives.

But consider this for a moment. Did you grow the food that sustains you every day? Did you till the soil, milk the cow, gather the eggs, kill the chicken? Did you make the car or train that takes you to work? Did you make the road? Extract the fuel? Sew your clothing? Build your house with lumber you milled? How do you live?

You need others every single day, every single moment of your life. It's thanks to others and their presence and effort that you have the things you need to continue, and that you have friendship and love and meaning in your life. Without others you have nothing. You may think, "Well, yes, but I work and I make money, and I pay for everything. So they are not taking care of me, it's my money that takes cares of me. Even the highways and commuter trains: I pay my taxes." But suppose you have a lot of money and there is no one else in the world but you, you and your gigantic pile of money. How would you survive? Could you eat the money? Could you make a house for yourself inside the money? The money is only valuable because others exist. Money makes no sense without others. Its value exists because others exist.

But our dependence on others runs even deeper than this. Where does the person we take ourselves to be come from in the first place? Apart from our parents' genes and their support and care, and society and all it produces for us, there's the whole network of conditions and circumstances that intimately makes us what we are. How about our thought and feeling? Where does it come from? Without words to think in, we don't think, we don't have anything like a sense of self as we understand it, and we don't have the emotions and feelings that are shaped and defined by our words. Did we invent this language that constitutes ourselves? No, it is the product of untold numbers of speakers over untold numbers of generations. Without the myriad circumstances that provided us the opportunities for education, for speech, for knowledge, for work, we wouldn't be here as we are. And without all the people in our lives whom we know and who know us and love us and create complications for us and infuriate us, we would have nothing to think about, we would be very bored. More than bored: without others our consciousness would be shattered by loneliness.

So it is literally the case that there could not be what we call a person without other people. We can say "person" as if there could be such an autonomous thing, but in fact there is no such thing. There is no such thing as a person. There are only persons who have cocreated one another over the long history of our species. The idea of an independent, isolated, atomized person is impossible. And here we are not only speaking of our needing others practically. We are talking about our inmost sense of identity. Our consciousness of ourselves is never independent of others.

This is what nonself or emptiness means in Buddhist teaching: that there is no such thing as an isolated individual. Though we can say there is, and though we might think there is, and though many of our thoughts and motivations seem to be based on this idea, in fact it is an erroneous idea. Literally every thought in our minds, every emotion that we feel, every word that comes out of our mouth, every material sustenance that we need to get through the day, comes through the kindness of and the interaction with others. And not only other people but nonhumans too, literally the whole of the earth, the soil, the sky, the trees, the air we breathe, the water we drink. We not only depend on all of this, we are all of it and it is us. This is no theory, no poetic religious teaching. It is simply the bald fact of the matter.

So to practice **Be grateful to everyone** is to train in this profound understanding. It is to cultivate every day this sense of gratitude, the happiest of all attitudes. Unhappiness and gratitude simply cannot exist in the same moment. If you feel grateful, you are a happy person. If you feel grateful for what is possible for you in this moment, no matter what your challenges are, grateful, first, that you are alive at all, that you can think, that you can feel, that you can stand, sit, walk, talk—if you feel grateful, you are happy and you maximize your chances for well-being and for sharing happiness with others.

These first three slogans, **Turn all mishaps into the path, Drive all blames into one,** and **Be grateful to everyone,** are relative bodhicitta slogans. That is, slogans that depend on a conventional understanding of beings as we usually conceive of them, self and other, you and I, them and us. The three go together: grateful to everyone and everything, we are willing to acknowledge whatever happens as an opportunity, which we accept with complete responsibility and receive with joy.

The fourth slogan, **See confusion as Buddha and practice emptiness,** requires a bit of explanation. This is a slogan of absolute bodhicitta, which, we will recall, goes beyond our conventional or relative understanding to a deeper sense of what we are. It is not dissimilar to what I have just been writing about: the impossibility of an isolated self, or in other words, the emptiness of the concepts of self and other. Though conventionally I am me and you are you, from an absolute perspective, a God's-eye view, if you will, there is no self and other. There's only Being, and there's only Love, which is Being sharing itself with itself without impediment and with warmth. It just happens to look like you and me to us, because this is how our minds and sensory apparatus works. This love without boundary is "emptiness practice."

**See confusion as Buddha and practice emptiness** means that we practice situating ourselves differently with respect to our ordinary human confusion, our resistance, our pain, our fear, our grief, and so on. Rather than hoping these emotions and reactions will eventually go away and we will be free of them, we take them to a deeper level. We look at their underlying reality. What is actually going on when we are upset or angry? What is happening? If we could unhook ourselves for a moment from the blaming and the wishing and the self-pitying and could look instead at the actual basis of what is in fact going on, what would we see? We would see time passing. We would see things changing. We would see life arising and passing away, coming from nowhere and going nowhere. Moment by moment, time slips away and things transform. The present becomes the past—or does it become the future? And yet right now there is no past or future. As soon as we examine "now" it is gone. And we cannot know how or where it goes. This may sound like philosophy, but it doesn't feel like philosophy when you or someone close to you is giving birth. If at that moment you are standing in the delivery room or are yourself, in pain and joy, giving birth—in that first bursting-forth moment, you are amazed. This small life you think you have been living, with its various issues and problems, completely disappears in the face of the miracle of visceral life springing forth in front of your eyes. Or if you are present when someone leaves this world and enters death (if there is such a place to enter), breathes his or her last and is gone, you know then that this emptiness is not just philosophy. You may not know what it is, but you will know that it is real. And that this reality is powerful and makes you see your life, and the whole of life, quite differently in that moment. A new context emerges that is more than thought, more than concept. When you view your daily human problems in the light of actual birth and actual death, you are practicing with this slogan. Every moment of your life, even (and maybe especially) your moments of pain or despair or confusion, is a moment of Buddha.

So do attend births and deaths whenever you can and accept these moments as gifts, opportunities for deep spiritual practice. But even when you aren't participating in these peak moments, you can repeat and review this slogan, and you can meditate on it. And when your mind is confused and entangled, you can take a breath and try to slip below the level of your desire and confusion. You can notice that in this very moment time is passing, things are transforming, and this impossible fact is profound, beautiful, joyful, even as you continue with your misery.

The fifth slogan:

**Do good, avoid evil, appreciate your lunacy, pray for help.**

Once again the slogans are bringing us back down to earth. If spiritual teachings are to really transform our lives, they need to oscillate (as the slogans do and are now doing again) between two levels, the profound and the mundane. If practice is too profound, it's no good: we are full of wonderful inspiring, lofty thoughts, insights, and speculations but lack the ability to get through the day with any gracefulness or to relate to the issues and people in ordinary life. We may be soaringly metaphysical, movingly compassionate, and yet unable to relate to a normal human or a worldly problem. This is the moment when the Zen master whacks us with her stick and says, "Wash your bowls! Kill the Buddha!" On the other hand, if practice is too mundane, if we become too interested in the details of how we and others feel and what we or they need or want, then the natural loftiness of our hearts will not be accessible to us, and we will sink under the weight of obligations, details, and daily-life concerns. This is when the master says, "If you have a staff, I will give you a staff; if you need a staff, I will take it away." We need both profound religious philosophy and practical tools for daily living. This double need, according to circumstances, seems to go with the territory of being human. We have just been contemplating reality as Buddha and practicing emptiness. That was important. Now it's time to get back down to earth.

First, do good. Do positive things. Say hello to people, smile at them, tell them happy birthday, I am sorry for your loss, is there something I can do to help? These things are normal social graces, and people say them all the time. But to *practice* them intentionally is to work a bit harder at actually meaning them when you do them, to actually cultivate a sense of caring and feeling for someone else that is as real as you can make it, paying attention to what you say, how you say it, and how you actually feel it or don't feel about it. We genuinely try to be helpful and kind and thoughtful in as many small and large ways as we can every day. From a religious point of view, doing good also includes wholesome religious acts like chanting a sacred text, studying, meditating, or giving money and other gifts to the spiritual community. All of these intentional positive actions, directly religious and not, generate virtue. They create a positive attitude in the mind or heart that will strengthen us for the good. In the Zen practice of Sixteen Bodhisattva Precepts, "doing good" corresponds to the second of the Three Pure Precepts: Cultivate What's Wholesome.

The second of the four practices listed in this slogan corresponds to the first of the Three Pure Precepts: Refrain from what's unwholesome. Or, simply put, avoid evil. This means to pay close attention to our actions of body, speech, and mind, noticing when we do, say, or think things that are harmful or unkind. Having come this far with our mind training, we can't help but notice our shoddy or mean-spirited moments. And when we notice them, we feel bad. In the past we might have said to ourselves, "I only said that because she really needs straightening out; if she hadn't done that to me, I wouldn't have said that to her. That's why I did it, it really was her fault." But now we see that this was a way of protecting ourselves (after all, we have just been practicing **Drive all blames into one**) and are willing to accept responsibility for what we have done. I'm not speaking here of terrible things. Most of us probably do not do terrible things on purpose. This practice mostly references small things, unkind thoughts or words that do not seem so bad and yet erode our sense of integrity if we don't pay attention to them. So we do pay attention to what we say, think, and do, not obsessively, not with a perfectionistic flair, but just as a matter of course and with generosity and understanding, and finally we purify ourselves of most of our ungenerous thoughts and words.

The last two practices in this slogan (which I have interpreted as "appreciate your lunacy" and "pray for help") traditionally have to do with making offerings to two kinds of creatures, demons (beings who are preventing you from keeping determined with your practice) and Dharma Protectors (beings who are helping you to remain true to your practice). Making offerings is an important practice in Indo-Tibetan Buddhism and also in Zen: we typically offer incense and chant sutras as offerings in rituals and daily services. But for our purposes now it is better to see these practices more broadly.

We can understand *making offerings to demons* as "appreciate your lunacy." Bow to your own weakness, your own craziness, your own resistance. Congratulate yourself for them, appreciate them. Truly it is a marvel, the extent to which we are selfish, confused, lazy, resentful, and so on. We come by these things honestly. We have been well trained to manifest them at every turn. This is the prodigy of human life bursting forth at its seams, it is the effect of our upbringing, our society, which we appreciate even as we are trying to tame it and bring it gently round to the good. So we make offerings to the demons inside us, we develop a sense of humorous appreciation for our own stupidity. We are in good company! We can laugh at ourselves and everyone else.

*Making offerings to Dharma Protectors:* we pray to whatever forces we believe or don't believe in for help. Whether we imagine a deity or a God or not, we can reach out beyond ourselves and beyond anything we can objectively depict and ask for assistance and strength for our spiritual work. We can do this in meditation, with silent words, or out loud, vocalizing our hopes and wishes. Prayer is a powerful practice. It is not a matter of abrogating our own responsibility. We are not asking to be absolved of the need to act. We are asking for help and for strength to do what we know we must do, with the understanding that though we must do our best, whatever goodness comes our way is not our accomplishment, our personal production. It comes from a wider sphere than we can control. In fact, it is counterproductive to conceive of spiritual practice as a task that we are going to accomplish on our own. After all, haven't we already practiced **Be grateful to everyone**? Haven't we learned that there is no way to do anything alone? We are training, after all, in *spiritual* practice, not personal self-help (though we hope it helps us, and probably it does). So not only does it make sense to pray for help, not only does it feel powerfully right and good to do so, it is also important to do this so that we remember that we are not alone and we can't do it by ourselves. It would be natural for us to forget this point, to fall into our habit of imagining an illusory self-reliance. People often say that Buddhists don't pray because Buddhism is an atheistic or nontheistic tradition that doesn't recognize God or a Supreme Being. This may be technically so, but the truth is Buddhists pray and have always prayed. They pray to a whole panoply of buddhas and bodhisattvas. Even Zen Buddhists pray. Praying does not require a belief in God or gods.

**Do good, avoid evil, appreciate your own lunacy, and pray for help!** Simple everyday instructions.

The sixth slogan is: **Whatever you meet is the path.**

Like the final slogan that closes the second point, this one sums up all the others under the heading of the third point: whatever happens, good or bad, make it part of your spiritual practice.

In spiritual practice, which is our life, there are no breaks and no mistakes. We human beings are always doing spiritual practice, whether we know it or not. You may think that you lost the thread of your practice, that you had been going along quite well and then life got busy and complicated and you lost track of what you were doing. You may have been embarrassed about this, felt bad about it, and that feeling fed on itself, and it became harder and harder to get back on track. And you think you are very far from your best intentions.

But this is just what you think, it's not what's going on. Once you begin practice (and if you have gotten this far in this book, you have begun), you always keep going, because everything is practice, even the days or the weeks or the months or decades or entire lifetimes when you forgot to meditate, forgot to pay attention to your spiritual thoughts and exercises. Even then you're still practicing, because it's impossible to be lost. You are constantly being found whether you know it or not. To practice this slogan, to memorize it, to repeat it to yourself again and again, to bring it up in meditation, to post it on your refrigerator, to keep it in mind, is to know that no matter what is going on, no matter how distracted you think you are, no matter how much you feel like a terribly lazy individual who has completely lost track of her good intentions and is now hopelessly astray—even then you are on the path and you have the responsibility and the ability to take all of that negative chatter and turn it into the path.

# 5

# Make Practice Your Whole Life

BEFORE BEGINNING our discussion of point four, a short review is in order.

We take our point of view so much for granted, as if the world were really as we see it. But it doesn't take much analysis to recognize that our way of seeing the world is simply an old unexamined habit, so strong, so convincing, and so unconscious we don't even see it as a habit. How many times have we been absolutely sure about someone's motivations and later discovered that we were completely wrong? How many times have we gotten upset about something that turned out to have been nothing? Our perceptions and opinions are often quite off the mark. The world may not be as we think it is. In fact, it is virtually certain that it is not.

There's nothing wrong with habits as such. Habits can be good. But in this case, a little reflection shows us that our habitual way of seeing things is not only not optimal, in many instances, large and small, it causes us much difficulty. It's often distorted, causing us extra upset we don't need, and it's too narrow, limiting our possibilities and our love. And yet we are pretty stuck on our point of view. Clearly, it will take some doing to see through it, and this is why spiritual practice takes time, effort, support, and much repetition. But little by little our way of seeing the world and being in it can shift. With effort, the mind can be trained. That is the underlying assumption of this book.

Mind training begins (point one, **Resolve to begin**) with our getting in touch with our deepest, best motivation. As human beings we are *inherently* motivated to see life truly and generously. This is our human birthright, our human capacity. It is why every human community from the dawn of time to the present has had some form of wholesome and salvific spirituality. But the pressures of life and the persistence of human folly, embedded as these are in our societies and our communities (and therefore also in our own minds and hearts), have obscured this motivation in us. So our course of training begins with getting in touch with our best motivation. (I will note here what the reader will already have noticed: that mind training isn't a linear matter. We don't fully complete one step and go on to the next. We are constantly working on all the steps, partially completing one and then having to go back to it, and all the others, again and again, in circular fashion, which is why a review at this point is probably realistic.)

Point two, **Train in empathy and compassion,** awakens our willingness to be with our own suffering and the suffering of others. Most of us believe suffering is negative, difficult, and to be avoided at all costs. Suffering breaks our spirit and ruins our life. So rather than face the suffering, we blame others or the world for the unfortunate things that have happened to us. Or we blame ourselves, imagining that we are essentially incapable of happiness and right action. All of this amounts to a strategy of distraction. Blame is a way of avoiding the actual suffering we feel. And if we are unwilling to face our own suffering, how much more are we unwilling to take in the suffering of others, let alone the whole mass of suffering of this troubled world. There is no way we could even entertain such a thought.

But the training proposes that we do exactly that. That we take in our own suffering, the suffering of our friends, of our communities, and of the world, because nothing is more effective than this to change our habitual point of view. We develop this capacity with the practice of sending and receiving, which begins with our willingness to receive and heal our own pain. Of course our efforts to do this will encounter powerful resistance within us. Suffering breeds resistance and loves it, loves our fear, gobbles it up, becoming bigger and stronger. The more we try to push away the suffering, the more difficult it is to bear. But through the practice of sending and receiving, repeated patiently over time, we discover that when we stop resisting, we can bear the suffering with much more equanimity than we previously thought possible. The monster you run away from in the dark becomes more and more frightening the faster and further you flee. The monster you face in your own house becomes a pussycat, which sometimes scratches and sometimes makes a mess on the floor, but you love her anyway. We discover we don't have to be afraid of suffering, that we can transform it into healing and love. And this is not as hard to do as we might have thought. Whatever our state, whatever our capacity, we can do it. We need only start from where we are and go as far as we can.

Doing this, we discover that our practice (and our life) isn't about—and has never been about—ourselves. As long as spiritual practice (and life) remains only about you, it is painful. Of course, your practice does begin with you. It begins with self-concern. You take up practice out of some need or some desire or pain. But the very self-concern pushes you beyond self-concern. Zen master Dogen writes, "To study Buddhism is to study the self, to study the self is to forget the self." When you study yourself thoroughly, this is what happens: you forget yourself, because the closer you get to yourself, the closer you get to life and to the unspeakable depth that is life, the more a feeling of love and concern for others naturally arises in you. To be self-obsessed is painful. To love others is happy. Loving others inspires us to take much better care of ourselves, as if we were our own mother. We take care of ourselves so that we can benefit others.

In this spirit we realize (point three, **Transform bad circumstances into the path**) that we no longer have to strategize constant self-protection, as we have been doing all of our lives. We see that suffering doesn't have to be so frightening, that we can make use of it to deepen and strengthen our life. This changes everything. We are now capable of making use of whatever happens to us, the good as well as the bad, and no longer have to be anxious and constantly obsessed with making sure we get what we want and avoid what we don't want, that we always win and never lose. Now we are free to win and free to lose. So we live with a lot less fear and anxiety. And even though the usual stuff keeps on coming (fear, avoidance, and so on), we have a new attitude toward it. We are more patient and accepting—and even appreciative—of our own foibles. Like everyone else, we struggle sometimes. Like everyone else, our lives are colorful, sad, and sometimes painful. But they are beautiful, and we're living them with others.

With this, we are ready for point four, **Make practice your whole life.**

This point is both an effort that we make going forward and a result of what we have already done.

People often complain to me that they don't have time for spiritual practice. In today's busy world, it seems that we can barely cover the basics, let alone refine our lives further with spirituality. When spiritual practice is an item at the bottom of our long to-do lists (which are these days embedded in task-accomplishment apps on our smartphones), it is very hard to get to it, and usually we don't. My answer to this is simple: spiritual practice is not an item on the list. It is not a task we do. It is *how* we do what we do. It's a spirit, an attitude. You are breathing all day long. It doesn't take any more time to be conscious, let's say, of three breaths in a row. Your mind is thinking distractedly all day long. It doesn't take any more time to intentionally think of a slogan you are working with. Even meditation practice, which seems to take time you ordinarily would be filling with some other activity, actually takes much less time when you realize how much time you save when your mind is a bit calmer and more focused and when your day begins with processing and settling with your life rather than rushing headlong into today with yesterday as yet undigested. Practice, in the light of this point, is not something we are doing over and above our life. It *is* our life. It is the way we live.

In Zen, traditional training expresses and extends this point. The template of the Zen life is the monastery, where you meditate when it's time to do that, eat when it's time to eat, walk when walking, talk when talking, sleep when sleeping. In other words, you do what you are doing fully, wholeheartedly, constantly trying to pay attention and be present. You use the task at hand as the meditation object, just coming back over and over again to where you are and to what is going on, just as, in meditation, you come back over and over again to the breath, without worry or fuss. As the great master Zhaozhou answered when asked about the process and meaning of spiritual practice, "Have you eaten? Then wash your bowls!"

For contemporary Zen practitioners, the template of the monastery can be applied in the tasks of daily living. We all eat, sleep, walk, work, and so on. It doesn't take extra time to do these things in the spirit of spiritual practice. **Making practice your whole life** can be seen as a simple matter of mindfulness.

Simply doing whatever you are doing with awareness, carefulness, and love. And when you notice you are not doing this, coming back to it. Theoretically, there is no reason why anyone can't do this, all of the time. Realistically, our habits are strong, and we probably need as much support as we can get to encourage us and keep us on the beam. (I hope this book is one such support.)

There are two slogans under this point. The first is:

### 17. Cultivate a serious attitude (traditionally: Practice the five strengths).

Probably our biggest challenge in spiritual practice is not that we don't have the time or the talent or the focus or the right atmosphere or setting. Probably the biggest challenge is simply that we don't take ourselves seriously enough. Though we may believe that spiritual practice is a good idea and self-transformation a possibility, when it comes down to it, we don't really think it's possible for *us*. Or maybe we actually don't *want* to transform. Of course we want to transform. Especially if our lives are noticeably unsatisfactory. But at the same time, we don't. Our motivations are mixed. So we can't be truly serious about our practice. This circles us back again to the first point, **Resolve to begin,** which asks us to reflect on our life in order to rediscover our best motivation. Here, in slogan 17, we are given another aid to finding and strengthening our motivation, the *Five strengths*, a traditional list of practices designed for just this purpose. The *Five strengths* are:

1. *Strong determination*
2. *Familiarization*
3. *Seed of virtue*
4. *Reproach*
5. *Aspiration*

**Strong determination** is exactly what it sounds like. It is a practice to teach us how to take ourselves seriously as dignified spiritual practitioners. To feel as if, whatever our shortcomings (and it is absolutely necessary that we are honest, even brutally honest, about our shortcomings at every point), we also have within us a powerful energy to accomplish the spiritual path. And that we do want to do this: it is of all things the most important thing for us.

When you stop to think about it, what *are* you after in your life, anyway? What is it that you most would like to accomplish or manifest with this one short, precious life you have been given? Of course you want to love and take care of your family and accomplish something in this world. You want to be someone, have some kind of identity in the world. We all need this and all it entails, in whatever way is possible for us to establish it. But why? Because we want to be good people, we want to fulfill our highest human destiny.

At our best, we all have high purposes, noble goals, even if we are modest about them. But we forget them. The daily grind takes us far from our reasons for doing what we do. We get lost in the details, absorbed in the problems. To practice strong determination is to intentionally stay connected to our higher goals and to remind us that we truly are spiritual practitioners, we are heroes, we can make effort, we can do what needs to be done to live a noble life.

To make this into a concrete practice, you could compose a short speech for yourself to this effect. Don't be afraid to be forthright and resolute about it and to use bold language. "Well, I might look like a merely ordinary person, but I am not. I am a spiritual warrior, a spiritual hero, and though this may not be apparent to others, inside it is clear to me. I definitely will be a sage! Maybe it will take a long time, maybe I won't complete the job in this lifetime. But there's no doubt about it whatsoever. I'm no longer committed as I was before to be stuck with my ordinary limited point of view; I'm leaving that behind. I'm going forward!" That's the spirit of *Strong determination*. So compose a speech like this for yourself and repeat it to yourself from time to time. In meditation, on the commuter train, whenever you can.

The second strength builds on this first one. With *Familiarization*, with repetition and repeated drill, comes the establishment of a new habit that is not, like the old ones, unconscious but instead is a habit you have thought about and chosen to cultivate for reasons that come out of your best motivations. *Familiarization* is brain washing, washing out an otherwise musty brain, freshening it up. Left alone with its unconscious habits, the mind goes down predictably dull and often disadvantageous pathways. We think, feel, and see in a way that doesn't serve us very well—and we assume that this is a fixed and necessary experience. It's not! *Familiarization* is repetition of teachings and intentional practices for the purpose of establishing new pathways, new habits. As we've said, the brain is plastic, fluid, it changes with our inner and outer activity. When we go to the gym to lift weights or do aerobics, we know that these activities are not something we will do once or twice. Their virtue is in the drill, the repetition over time; this is what changes our body. With *Familiarization* the habits we want to inculcate will little by little become automatic. When someone asks you for your address or phone number, you probably don't say, "Let me think about it." You don't need to reflect or consult with anyone. The information is at the tip of your tongue because you are fully familiar with it. You haven't needed to make a special study of the information, because by simple repetition with interest over time you have made these facts part of you. The same thing happens with spiritual practice. Faith, God, and inspiration aside, repetition is the true soul of spirituality.

This is a sad fact: If someone does ask you for your phone number, your address, your bank account, your place of business, and so on, you can answer easily because these things are uppermost in your mind. You refer to them every day. But if someone asks you to account for the condition of your soul, probably your response would not be at the tip of your tongue. Probably you would be embarrassed or confused by the question. How good is it that we are quite familiar with our outer circumstances and activities but quite unfamiliar with our inner lives, with our soul, our spirit? The practice of *Familiarization* proposes that we correct this imbalance and become just as fluent in our spiritual lives as we are in our material lives.

*Seed of virtue* is the recognition of our noble heritage as human beings. As we discussed under the first point, it's a rare and precious thing to be a human being. We all understand this. This is why we send money overseas in times of disaster, why we know it is wrong to take a human life. Not just because it is illegal. Because human life is sacred, precious. The heritage, the legacy, of being human is to manifest wisdom, compassion, and loving-kindness, to be fully worthy of our lives, worthy of admiration and celebration. This is your nature, my nature, the nature of every human being. In this we are all the same. No one is more worthy, more sacred, than you are. And you are no more worthy, or sacred, than anyone else.

Given this as a basis for our life, we can be perfectly aware of our many faults. Faults are perfectly natural, like earthquakes or floods. They may have bad consequences sometimes, but they are to be expected. The more we can learn to anticipate their periodic eruptions, the better off we will be.

But along with these various faults, at the same time, deep

within us is this beautiful human heritage. The virtue of our great saints and spiritual exemplars the world over is not to set up their supposed perfection as a reproach to us. It is the opposite. Their example shows us what we could be and what we are. To practice *Seed of virtue* is to remind ourselves every day of who we really are. None of the world's great spiritual exemplars has ever said, "Look at me, how great I am, pay attention to me!" All have said, "I am what you are."

The Dalai Lama is fond of saying, "I'm just a simple monk, I'm trying my best," and I believe he really means this. He's trying his best to practice. And if we admire him, what we are really admiring is not him but this potential within ourselves. To cultivate this attitude is the third strength, *Seed of virtue.*

The fourth strength, *Reproach,* is not so easy to understand or to practice, because it is so close to something we do all the time that's not very helpful. Here is a case in which the Buddhist or traditional Asian viewpoint is so different from our contemporary way of looking at things that we have to be very precise and clear with how we understand and work with this slogan.

We are all, of course, quite familiar with reproach: we reproach ourselves and others constantly; we are quite good at being critical, even hypercritical. *Judgmental,* as we say. Which we take not to be a good thing. But the practice of *Reproach* is precisely that we be judgmental. But how, and with what attitude and purpose?

We have generally, most of us, a very low sense of respect for ourselves. So we feel that we cannot afford to be critical of ourselves for fear that we'll immediately become vicious. So we do the next best thing: we blame someone else, turning our viciousness on him or her. Or maybe we are beyond this, and as good spiritual people we make a practice of not blaming others. Instead we are merciless with ourselves.

But if you have practiced *Strong determination,* if you have practiced *Familiarization,* if you have cultivated the *Seed of virtue,* you can have a much more affectionate relationship with your imperfect self. And you can view yourself with much more generosity, just as you would a child you were trying to teach.

If we are honest we have to admit that we have a lot of bad habits that keep appearing over and over again, despite all of our good intentions. Of course! Look at all we've been through! Look at our crazy parents! Look at this troubled world we're living in! If we are wrecks inside, it's no mystery why. It's the most natural thing in the world. But it's okay, because we know that underneath that, we have a sacred noble human nature. In that spirit and with that knowledge we can correct ourselves without brutality or aggression. We can complain to ourselves ("Hey, you did it again! Cut that out! Stop that! What's the matter with you?") and still maintain a gentleness and sense of humor.

Generally we judge ourselves and others for their essential character. This is why when we are judgmental we feel so guilty or so full of condemnation and contempt. But in the practice of **Reproach** it's as if we were creating the bad habit, the greed or anger or selfishness, *to be a person in its own right.* And it's that person, not ourselves or someone else, that we reproach.

With regard to ourself, for example, we may try to become as familiar as we can with some of our most popular bad habits. Take jealousy, for instance. Instead of being spun around by our jealousy, confused and full of passion and self-blame, as if the jealousy were somehow a substance ingrained in our essential character, that it was part of us, we study the jealousy. We become curious, almost scientific about it. How does it feel inside? How does it cause us to think and want to act? We study the jealousy until we can see it as a kind of entity, as if it were an independent person rather than a part of ourselves. And then we can reproach the jealousy. "Here you are again, my skillful, silly old opponent. Many times you have fooled me and taken me in, but not this time! I reproach you with all my heart! I see you but I am not taken in!" The jealousy is not us, it is not ourselves, it is simply something very disadvantageous that is arising. We don't have to be so convinced by it and we don't have to take it so personally .

In his commentary on this slogan, the great Tibetan master Trungpa Rimpoche spoke of making speeches to our various bad habits: To our selfishness, for instance, we could say, "You know, you are a terrible person, you have caused me so much trouble, I'm so tired of you, and you know I just don't like you anymore! It's all because of you that I have all of these problems, and you know what? I'm not going to hang around with you anymore! And who are you anyway? I'm fed up, go away! I have absolutely no use for you at all!"

To be able to address your own selfishness like this would be quite unusual. Because this is exactly *not* how we view our various faults. We don't think of our selfishness as being an opponent, an adversary in its own right. We do think of it as ours and that we ought to be ashamed of it. The idea that my selfishness is somehow an independent entity that I can reproach and disidentify with doesn't come naturally to me.

And yet, if I think about it for a moment, why not? My experience shows me that my life consists of experiences that are constantly coming and going. As we discussed earlier, even my sense of self is something that comes and goes; there is no place it exists and no particular experience or substance I can point to that is "me." I can think this through, but even more, my daily meditation practice has given me the visceral experience that it is certainly so. There is no *essential* me. Things are coming and going, here, within the sphere of what I call my consciousness, and that is all. So it really is true—my jealousy isn't mine and isn't me. I am responsible for *dealing* with it—which I do by practicing **Reproach.** But I am not responsible for its being there; it just arises, and it isn't really mine. It's not necessary at this point in our training that we completely grasp this point. We will grasp it eventually, little by little, as we continue. The training itself will show us that we don't have to take everything so personally. That we can have a much more flexible and even humorous attitude toward ourselves and our many faults than we ever thought possible. And once our attitude loosens up, everything becomes much more workable.

The fifth strength, *Aspiration,* is vow or commitment. I referred earlier to the Four Bodhisattva Vows in Zen practice. These are traditionally chanted by the assembly after a dharma talk, and I often wonder what people are thinking as they intone "Beings are numberless, I vow to save them; delusions are inexhaustible, I vow to end them; Dharma gates [entrances to the practice] are boundless, I vow to enter them; Buddha's Way is unsurpassable, I vow to become it." These are certainly very impractical commitments. In fact, they are literally, precisely impossible to fulfill. But why not have aspirations so lofty they are impossible to fulfill? To have aspirations any less lofty would be to sell ourselves short. The trick is to keep on making effort in the direction of fulfillment of the aspiration but not to think that you will actually complete the job—and not to be dismayed or discouraged by this but instead to be encouraged by it. This is a good approach because you will always have more to do and always be spurred on by the strength of your commitment. To commit to something you actually could accomplish is such small potatoes for a lofty, sacred human being like yourself.

The Four Bodhisattva Vows are extravagant and enthusiastic, vows of one who is committed to bodhicitta, the aspiration to becoming awakened for the benefit of others (as we discussed earlier). While the word *bodhisattva* may be a Buddhist word, I think it stands for something more basically human. We all want to be compassionate, giving, loving people at the bottom of our hearts. This is a human, not a Buddhist, aspiration. We would all like to serve others, to feel for others, to love others with everything we've got. We would all like to be a light for the world.

We admire people who are wealthy, famous, or skillful in some way, but it's not hard to be like that. If you are born with some talent, a little luck, and you know the right people, you can do that. Many people do that. Much more difficult and much more wonderful is to be a bodhisattva. Not someone that many people know about and talk about but someone who has the almost magical power of spreading happiness and confidence wherever he goes. What a vision for your life, for your family, to be a light for those around you! To think of everything you do, every action, every social role, every task, as being just a cover for, an excuse for, your real aspiration, to be a bodhisattva, spreading goodness wherever you go. This requires no luck (even if everything goes wrong in your life, you can do it), no special skills, no need to meet special people and get special breaks. We can all do this. This is the aspiration we should all cultivate for training the mind.

There is one more slogan under this fourth point, and it is a very important one:

## 18. Practice for death as well as for life.

The first three points mostly have to do with practice under special circumstances, especially in difficult times, times of suffering or trouble. Compassion requires that we be able to face our own pain and the pain of others; turning difficult circumstances into the path also requires us to face difficulty and learn how to reverse the natural tendency to run away from rather than face what's hard. Since so many people identify spiritual practice with feeling good and having pleasant experiences, it is crucially important that our training begin with these realities.

Because if you can't practice when things are rough, if in difficulty you revert to old ways of being and doing, you are sunk,
and your practice isn't worth much.

But we could also go to the other extreme and focus so much
on suffering and pain and difficulty that we begin to imagine
spiritual practice as a grim process of facing one nasty moment
after another. It isn't that. There is plenty of joy and happiness
along the way—in fact, as we keep on, more and more happiness,
even when things go wrong and conditions are difficult. Spiritual
practice *does* make your life better, but only when you are willing
to do it for its own sake and give up a big focus on improvement.
This is the paradox: your life improves when you stop worrying
about improvement.

But notice that all of this is about your *life* in good times or
bad. If you think about religion, why it exists, what function it
has in human cultures and in individual lives, you will soon run
past life into larger and more mysterious questions. In fact, spiritual practice in particular, and religion in general, wouldn't exist
if it weren't for the fact that we die, and we really don't know
how to understand, cope with, or digest this fact. So even though
we do spiritual practice while we are alive and for our lives, really, we do it because we die and in order to understand and cope
with death, grief, and loss.

In fact, it is artificial to separate life from death. In a very concrete and down-to-earth sense, there is no such thing as "life" or
"death." In Zen practice we speak of "birth-and-death" as being
one phenomenon, and of course it is. We have already discussed
this. Time passing is birth-and-death. Moments arise and then
pass away; this is one action, one moment. Loss is constant and
conditions our every thought, word, and deed. When I train
caregivers for the dying in spiritual hospice care, I always tell
them that the work they do isn't about death, it's about life. You
are alive as long as you are alive, and when you are not, you are

not. It's a mistake to think of a hospice patient as "dying." The patient is alive as long as she is alive. Truly, she is no more dying that we are. For we *are* dying. That's what living is: dying a little, moment after moment.

You could say that the whole point of spiritual practice is to prepare for death. One of my favorite sayings is by an obscure French writer named Charles Péguy, who wrote, "A person doesn't die from this or that disease. He dies from his whole life." This is certainly true. The way we live is the way we die.

This slogan is telling us that as much as we need to practice the *Five strengths* for our lives, just as much do we need to practice them for our deaths, and specifically at the time of our death. Many people become religious or spiritual as they near death. This makes a lot of sense. When you are in bed, maybe in pain and sensing your life is now short, you are not so concerned about how to live more successfully going forward. The imminence of death has a way of grabbing your attention and changing your priorities. Everybody pays attention to his or her inner life and to questions of meaning when death is coming close—unless, that is, the person were to deny that death is close, which some can do. Death is powerful, it is very immediate, it is a great motivator. But if you wait till the time when death is close to begin your practice, it may well be too late. It is much better to spend time in your life working on your spiritual practice so at the time of death it will be there for you. So that when you're dying, instead of being subject to a mind full of confusion and dread, it will be possible for you to meditate on love and compassion. And maybe even experience death (if this phrase makes any sense, it might not) as a process of entering unlimited love and compassion. Certainly I would never suggest to someone who is close to the end of life, "Well, have you thought of entering death as a field of unlimited love?" He may well answer me, "You're

full of crap, get out of here, I'm dying." But if we have spent time
in our life cultivating our spiritual practice, until, as this fourth
point suggests, we see our whole life as practice, then it may be
possible that our death can be not a tragedy but something much
more. I have seen this happen.

Even in the last moments of life, you can breathe in and you
can breathe out. You can breathe in the suffering and breathe out
healing and relief. And when your selfishness pops up with fear
and despair, you can turn around and say to it: "Ah, there you are
again. I've been telling you to get out of here for a long time, and
this time I really mean it, I'm going back to breathing, I'm going
back to my meditation on love and compassion, and you see that
glass of water on my bedside? You come back one more time, I'm
throwing it all over you!"

And then you can remember, as you breathe in and out, all
the things that you have been practicing for many years. You can
remember that life is like a dream, that it has only ever been
things coming and going, insubstantially, mysteriously. And that
whatever form your life will take from the time of death onward,
it will move in the same rhythm in which it has always moved.
Such experiences are actually possible. And if you are practicing
now with a resolution to continue, with strong determination,
with aspiration, with confidence in the *Seed of virtue,* perhaps
your practice will be there for you at the time of your own death.
And you will be able to bring your practice to the bedside of family members, loved ones, and friends when they are close to
death. You will be able to bring a sense of confidence and peace
to those most precious moments.

As I said at the outset, Zen practice is very simple: just breathe in,
breathe out. Just be where you are. You could say that the whole
edifice of the mind-training text we are following in this book

is just a long-winded way of saying: breathe in, breathe out, be where you are. All of these teachings come down to that. So simple, yet not so easy to do. We have so many complications!

Human beings are not just complex machines. Even though we now understand the lungs, the heart, the stomach, and so on, and can take apart and put together a human body and repair it in all kinds of previously unimagined ways, we know that a human being is not limited to his or her material hardware. We may understand a lot about what a human body is and how it works, but we understand very little about the soul, the spirit, the consciousness that illuminates that human body and makes it a living human being.

I have a nephew who is a cognitive scientist trying to understand the nature of consciousness. I asked him: "Have you figured it out?" He said: "Not only have we not figured it out, but we don't even know the question that we should ask yet so as to point us in a direction we could go to begin figuring it out. Or whether there is a question that we could ask, or a way to answer the question if we could ask it."

Breathing in and breathing out is an unspeakably deep process. To be alive is immense and unknowable. It's no accident that in Latin and Greek, and in Hebrew, English, and Spanish, and probably in many other languages, the word for *spirit* is *breath*.

# 6

## Assess and Extend

IF OUR FOURTH POINT was **Make practice your whole life,**
don't think of it as something extra, this fifth point is the necessary next step. Remember, we are talking about a process of
training. That is, envisioning your life as a process of opening
and growing rather than simply enduring what happens to you,
willy-nilly. If you are going to adopt a practice or training point of
view for your life, you will need a way of assessing, of seeing how
you are doing as the process unfolds. You will need feedback.

My wife is a middle school teacher. She is always giving her
students various kinds of quizzes and tests. Maybe the students
think of these unpleasant events as ways their worth or skill is
being evaluated. But my wife understands that the point of such
assessments is not to determine the students' worth or skill level.
The point is to check whether they are learning the material, and
if they are not, in what ways they are deficient. With that information, she can adjust and pinpoint her instruction so that learning—which is never perfect and never ends—can be maximized.
That's what this fifth point is about. It consists of four watch-
words, four slogans, for keeping you on the beam and giving you

tools to see how you are doing at any given point. Once you see how it's going, you can extend and refine your practice. (Again I caution the reader to go lightly. Do not fall into middle school mind. We are not worried about grades or even progress. We do not want to turn corrosive judgment on ourselves, which will produce discouragement. The point is simply to remain engaged and informed so we can keep on making a steady, solid, interested effort.)

This point consists of four slogans:

**19. There's only one point.**
**20. Trust your own eyes.**
**21. Maintain joy (and don't lose your sense of humor).**
**22. Practice when you're distracted.**

**There's only one point,** and it's so simple, however much we keep on forgetting it: Don't be so stuck on yourself! Open up! Mind training comes down to this. Keeping this slogan close by at all times is a good tool for seeing how you are doing. Whenever you feel upset, unhappy, dissatisfied, in a snit, frozen, constricted, bound—check and see. Probably if you reflect deeply enough, you'll come to the realization that the ultimate cause of this unpleasantness is that you are in one way or another stuck on yourself, favoring yourself and your own needs, desires, and viewpoint more than is necessary. Even recognizing this, and opening up just a little, relieves the pressure.

Think about it: you are living in a big world, with lots going on, many problems, many challenges, sad things, happy things. And all of this is the sphere of your life, it's the ocean you swim in, the air you breathe; you are not separate from it for even a moment. Why would you want to artificially, conceptually, remove yourself from life's great ocean and lock yourself up in the tiny prison of self, in which, despite your best efforts, you constantly feel confined and under attack? The whole of the practice comes down to this: stop being so stuck on yourself. Let go of that and open up. Think of others. Try to do something to make them happy. Anything: something small like "Hello, how are you?" And mean it. This is a way to assess your practice as you go along, a question to ask yourself on a regular basis: Am I less stuck on myself, more available to others than I used to be? Am I thinking positively and generously of others more often? Be honest about your answers to these questions. If you have to admit that no, you are not thinking more of others, you are just as stuck on yourself as you ever were, that's okay, that's information. You know what you have to do. Invite someone out to lunch. Ask someone how she is. Practice more sending and receiving.

You can also practice this slogan particularly when you are feeling tight and embattled. When you notice a sinking feeling inside, say to yourself: "There's only one point: open up!" Take three conscious breaths. Don't think something in particular is supposed to happen. This is training. It takes time. You just have to keep on repeating the process. So take those three breaths. Notice what happens, and whatever it is, go on.

**Trust your own eyes.**

With **Trust your own eyes,** we notice again something that has come up before: the slogans often seem to go counter to one another. There seems to be an unstated effort to balance one side with another. No sooner do we digest one slogan than the next slogan comes along pointing us in what seems to be the opposite direction. This is not mere perversion or trickery. It simply addresses one of the main features of our typical human folly: that we are likely to take a good thing too far, until it becomes a bad thing. Going to the left side of the road to avoid an obstacle, we go too far left and fall into the ditch. Now we have to go right. But if we go too far right, we might fall into the ditch on the other side of the road, so we have to go left again. We saw this when we studied absolute bodhicitta in chapter 2. There we had the slogans **See everything as a dream** and **Examine the nature of awareness.** Practicing these made us feel dreamy, cooled out, and a bit abstracted from the rough and tumble of the ordinary interactive world. That was, to some extent, good. It was a good antidote to our embattled anxiety. But taken too far, it made us too removed, too cooled out. So we had to come back. The next slogan, **Don't get stuck on peace,** was an antidote for this condition. We could recognize, when we felt annoyed that others were disturbing our profound Buddhist peacefulness, our dream-like awareness, that maybe there was something a bit off, and we remembered **Don't get stuck on peace,** which brought us back to ordinary life, where we belong.

Here we see the same thing in operation. Having just heard that we should open up and not be so stuck on ourselves, not insist on seeing everything from our own point of view, and that instead we should think of others, expand our lives, we now hear, **Trust your own eyes.** Only you can determine what is happening in your life and what to do about it.

The original wording of the Indo-Tibetan text is something like, "Of the two witnesses, hold the principal one." "The two witnesses" refers to the two witnesses of your life: you, and everyone else. The principal witness is you.

Recall that this fifth point is about assessing and extending your practice. Practice is not a blunt instrument, it's subtle and sensitive. Slogans are slogans, but they have to be applied with delicacy. What's good medicine for one person is poison for another; what's right in one situation is wrong in another; what works today may not work tomorrow. Life is full of nuance and indeterminacy. In order to assess what is going on and know what to do, you must constantly adjust and refine. You must always be ready to rethink and reset. You must avoid the masochistic habit of knocking your head repeatedly against a wall. Feeling yourself doing that is a sure sign that it is time to take a breath and ask yourself what is going on.

In this process of creatively training your mind, where does your feedback come from? Who or what do you trust to keep you on track? This slogan tells you to trust yourself. Of the two witnesses, trust the principal one, which is you.

Human subjectivity, the feeling we all have (and take completely for granted) of being a person, is one of the most marvelous and mysterious phenomena on the planet. Though cognitive scientists like my nephew are hard at work studying and marveling at it, no one really understands it. And no one really knows how it feels to be you. The actual inner climate of what it's like to be the unique person that you are is unknown to every other person. And that's why, in the final analysis, only you can evaluate and understand your own practice.

Of course, you don't want to be stubborn about it. You don't want to ignore everybody else. Others' views and feedback are essential. Very often others see you more clearly than you see yourself. Still, it is your responsibility and yours alone to see your life as clearly as possible and to act on what you see. No one else can do this for you, even if someone else has a wiser and clearer viewpoint on you than you do. If that's so, if there's someone who sees you better than you can see yourself, even so, it's you and only you who can decide to take up that viewpoint and make it your own. It's not the opinion of others about you that, in the final analysis, matters; it's your own sense of your life that makes your life. If you give over that responsibility, then you become a wobbly person, constantly looking to the right and to the left to see what you are supposed to be doing and thinking.

So it really is impossible for anyone else to diminish you or to elevate you. If other people's opinions diminish or elevate you, it's only because you have vacated your own opinions. No one likes to be criticized, disrespected, or judged by others in an uncomplimentary light. But when it comes to basic self-worth, only you are the judge. But judgment is a tricky thing. Trusting the principal witness, one's self, doesn't mean allowing yourself to be again the victim of self-judgment. Self-judgment, as we usually experience it, is corrosive and unhelpful.

What is self-judgment anyway? If you study it, you will see that most of the time it involves comparison: one's self is unworthy compared with others, who seem to be perfectly fine. We feel our inadequacy in relation to others—we imagine how others would judge us, and we internalize those judgments. Self-judgment doesn't actually come from the principal witness. It is a sneakily internalized function of outside forces. The principal witness is the self that is not self-condemnatory, the self that loves itself and is absolutely trustworthy. It may well have a negative assessment of this or that, but this is a useful, not a crushing, assessment, however negative it may be. A low score on a science exam in middle school is not something one necessarily wants, but it is quite useful in the process of learning. So in practicing this slogan, watch out for the usual corrosive style of self-judgment. If it is there to excess, ask yourself, "Who is judging whom?" You can practice this right now, setting the book aside and stopping at this sentence.

"Who is judging whom?" Good question. The answer's not obvious. When you are under attack from self-judgment, ask this question again and again until you have found a bit of ease. This slogan is not, as it might seem on the surface, promoting conventional self-reliance. It is not opening the door to self-judgment. It is gently urging us to a profound sense of inner balance, to a deeper connection with the intimacy of mind.

There's a Zen practice slogan that might help us understand this: "When alone, practice as if you were with others, and when with others, practice as if you were alone." This is something I always try to practice. It's an act of imagination, as so many spiritual practices are. A sort of mental and emotional yoga.

When you're with others, try not to be an actor playing the part of yourself. I think it is entirely normal for us to play the role of ourselves when we're with others, although we don't realize we're doing this. We use the persona we take to be our social self as an unconscious way of distancing ourselves from our truer and more intimate selves. The slogan is suggesting that instead of doing that, we should try to imagine that other people are not other people, not outside our mind, not scary, and that they therefore do not require our performance. Imagine that others are actually parts of your own mind, not outside entities who need to be impressed or appeased. They are actually as intimate with you as you are with yourself. If you can figure out how to situate yourself with others imaginatively in this way, you can be very relaxed and easygoing, you can be trusting and unafraid, because being with others feels like being with yourself. There's no need to be special or distinguished in any way. You can just be genuine, say and do what you feel. If you can find your ease with this, you'll find that there's no need to censor yourself in any way. If your feeling is that others are you and you are they, your impulses will be socially acceptable and even kind. It is a great relief to practice like this. Social anxiety nearly disappears.

On the other hand, when you are alone, try not to sink into the usual dull subjectivity that comes when you imagine that no one is around, no one can see you, you're hiding, invisible, and so can safely be a dim-witted idiot, with the radio and television simultaneously playing as you whack mindlessly away at the keyboard of your computer or mobile device. To improve this quite accustomed state, imagine you're in the middle of a crowd, a crowd of good, kind, serious people who like you and inspire you to comport yourself with the same degree of dignity that they do. Surrounded by such people, naturally you feel at your best. You pay attention to what you are doing and you take care of things with appreciation as soon as they arise. Imagine feeling this way when you are alone, inspired and elevated by your own company!

It seems to me to be a special feature of our contemporary culture that we carry at the heart of our feeling of subjectivity a sense of shame or embarrassment. We feel uncomfortable with ourselves because of this, deeply uncomfortable, which is why we don't like being alone for very long. In long meditation retreats, I have noticed that people often feel quite uncomfortable when they get too close to confronting their own basic sense of being a person. Just that: being a person, nothing more. To get comfortable with it, they have to wade though quite a bit of shame, dread, and discomfort. This means that the sense we have about ourselves is not what our self actually feels like. This is an astonishing thing to contemplate: that the person we feel inside is a distortion of some kind, a bad habit. That this person is not actually ourselves; it's our self-clinging, our self-confusion that we're experiencing and calling our self. The actual human subjectivity, the true principal witness, is a miraculous experience. It is a great achievement of consciousness, this feeling we have of being a person. Practicing this slogan may be tricky, and we can't expect it to suddenly change the long habit of how we have been feeling about ourselves, but it is a start. It will shake things up a bit. It will show us where we are stuck and how to go forward.

**Maintain joy (and don't lose your sense of humor).**

How is practicing the slogan **Maintain joy** possible? Your mind is going to be joyful or it's not. How could you cause it to be joyful when you are in a bad mood? How could you keep your sense of humor when things are going badly? How realistic is this in the sort of world we live in, being the people we are?

But on further reflection, it may not be so absurd. Remember, this is the *fifth* point of our training. Presumably by this time we have some experience under our belts. Perhaps by now we have learned to trust ourselves more, to be able to be honest about our shortcomings without condemning ourselves for them. Maybe by now we've gotten the hang of how to practice with difficulty. By now we really get it that running away inside doesn't work, it only compounds the trouble, and that we are capable of facing difficult emotions without so much denial and avoidance. Maybe at this point we've been working for a while with *Determination* and *Familiarization,* working on developing faith in our essential human goodness, on the practices of *Reproach, Aspiration,* and so on, as we've discussed. If so, it is likely that we are in a better mood more of the time than we have ever been, and a feeling of joy and gratitude isn't so foreign to us as it used to be. In fact, such feelings are never very far away. So we can begin to imagine that it is possible to keep and extend a joyful feeling, even when things are tough. We now know that conditions need not necessarily give rise to habitual reactions. To some extent, as we continue to train, we have more and more choice about how we respond to what happens to us. Bad conditions need not destroy our state of mind. Even in the darkest of moments, there's some light. We can maintain our sense of humor, our sense of ease. And this really helps, especially when things are grim. When, through your meditation and slogan practice, you have developed a habitual culture of awareness in your life; when the empty or boundless nature of things is always close at hand and is something that you think about, that you're aware of; when impermanence is no longer something you hate, it's your good friend—then yes, it is possible to maintain joy and humor most of the time.

Also, remember that this is a slogan for assessment. Working with it is not a matter of pressuring ourselves to feel joy all the time. When we aren't joyful, when we're depressed or bitter, we need to know that we feel that way, not cover it up with a veneer of fake spiritual joy because someone says we should. The point is that we assess our situation with this slogan **Maintain joy and humor.** We notice when this is so for us and when it's not, and we assume that when it's not, we have to pay attention and see how to adjust or work with our mind. **Maintain joy and humor** is a tool designed to help us, not a stick to beat ourselves up with or an invitation to pretend we are feeling what we actually are not feeling.

Here I can take myself as an example. I am not a model practitioner, far from it, but I have been doing the practice steadily since my youth, and it has given me more or less a fairly lighthearted attitude and a sense of humor about things, even though my natural state of mind is probably fairly dour. I'm still dour after all of these years, but I am fairly lighthearted about it! I don't work too hard at my practice, and yet as the years have gone on, I find that I am a happier guy despite advancing age and the loss of many good friends to death. I'm not so sure everyone who knows me would say this, but this is my honest assessment of my own inner state, as far as I know it and can recall.

Now suppose that suddenly, while I am innocently minding my own business, somebody jumps on me and starts beating me up. This has fortunately never happened to me, but it could. How would I react? Of course I don't really know, but judging from reactions I've had in the past when similar unexpected dangerous things have happened, I guess I'd be energetically impressed with the immediacy of what was going on and interested to see what was going to happen next. I suppose that spontaneously I'd try to defend myself somehow. But I do not think I would be surprised or in a panic. And if circumstances came to pass that caused me to lose everything—my health, my home, my spouse, my reasonably balanced state of mind (this last one has happened, of course, and more than once), and find myself suddenly in a total panic—well, this would be very startling. This would definitely get my attention, and I would be curious about how I was going to handle my out-of-control mind, what would happen, and there would be some joy in that I think, some spaciousness mixed in with the strong bad feeling. Maybe I'd be thinking, "Wow, I never thought this could happen! All of these years of expensive Zen training and look at me, I'm in a total panic. Practice has been getting too easy maybe. Now I am really going to test out all of this Zen teaching I have been yakking about all of these years and see if it really works." Probably that's how I'd maintain my joyful mind and my sense of humor. And insofar as I was brought low and lost my lightness and ease, I'm sure I'd notice that and realize I was in trouble and try to get some help if I could. I have a lot of friends and am confident that somehow someone would help me.

The last slogan is **Practice when you're distracted.** As we have been saying, we're in training, we're training the mind, and training takes discipline. We have to try to pay attention, to stick to our commitments, to repeat the training disciplines (the slogans) many times, keeping on with them even when we don't feel like it.

But discipline is not what we think it is. It's not an unpleasant yoke administered by a drill sergeant, an obsessed and mean-spirited guy who screams at us when we fall down on the job, or by a harsh, scary Zen master with his big stick. Aggressive discipline like this isn't very effective for most people. It usually inspires its opposite. Every force produces a counterforce, and the harsher the discipline, the more inspired we are to rebel.

The discipline of mind training isn't like this at all. It's gentle, permissive, and easygoing. Because of this, it doesn't inspire rebellion. In fact, mind training understands that distraction and noneffort or countereffort is inevitable and must be used as part of the effort we are making. We don't struggle against it, we cooperate with it. The discipline of mind training doesn't assume that relaxation and easygoing effort is counterproductive to the task or that it is possible for us to be on the beam all the time. The assumption is that we need to relax, we need to be spacious and open, and that this will help us train. Distraction isn't a problem. We have to learn how to practice even when we are distracted, to make the distraction part of the practice. Serving a cup of tea requires a certain kind of effort. If you are too tense, you'll pour too much into the cup, and grasping the cup with nervous fingers, you'll spill scalding tea all over yourself. Instead, you need to be loose and easy. On the other hand, if you are too loose and easy and aren't paying attention to what you're doing, you'll lose your grasp on the cup and drop it. Finding just the right amount of ease and looseness, not too much, not too little, is a key element in the training. We have to learn how to keep the thread of our training going even in lax times, even when we're daydreaming, losing track of ourselves, or enjoying the ball game or a glass of wine. We have to stop thinking that at times like that we have set our practice aside and are taking a break. That we are practicing when we are meditating or reciting the slogans and not when we are not. **Make practice your whole life.** There are no breaks. Or to put it another way, practice is just one long break from the tension and anxiety that we used to take for granted as the essential flavor of our lives.

There's another saying in Zen that I am very fond of: "When you fall down on the ground, you use the ground to get up." This is exactly what happens when you fall down. You use the ground for leverage to get up, you push off from the ground.

Again, I can use myself as an example. I usually sit in meditation in the morning while alone in my house. For many years I sat with others in official Zen meditation halls early in the morning. But now I consider my daily meditation relaxing and easygoing, a time of great ease and peacefulness. As I sit, my mind is often floating around like a cloud, this way and that way. Sometimes my mind is quiet and still, but a lot of times it's just floating like that.

You might say, "Poor fellow, he is so distracted." Maybe I am, but on the other hand, to me it seems a very beautiful thing to drift along with the mind that way, with all the various wonderful things that float into the mind and float out of the mind, with all the passions and the thoughts and feelings, and with the various stains from my lifetime, or someone's lifetime—sometimes it's not so clear whose.

You don't have to be perfect. You don't have to be on the beam every moment. Discipline isn't like that. There's a time for hard focus and a time for soft focus. It's not that practice is directed, serious, and important and that distractions are something else. Practice is life, including everything in your life, even the distractions. When you think you are distracted, when you think you have forgotten about your practice, remember this slogan: **Practice when you're distracted.** You may well be distracted. But there's nothing wrong with that. As soon as you know your state of distraction, you are practicing, you have remembered your practice. Distraction, laziness, indulging in stuck emotions like anger, jealousy, and so on, are all part of the practice. You fall down on the ground and you use the ground to get up. Using the ground to get up is remembering to notice the state you are in. As soon as you know your state, whatever that state is, you are practicing this slogan. You are back on the beam. You never actually lost track of it anyway. There are no distractions, after all.

# 7

## The Discipline of Relationship

REMEMBER THAT ALTHOUGH we're practicing fifty-nine slogans for generating compassion and resilience, compassion turns out not to be what it seems. There's much more to it than simply being nice and sympathetic to others. It's not that we are not trying to be nice and sympathetic to others; of course we aspire to be that way. But deeper reflection shows us that if we want to love and connect to others authentically, we have to liberate ourselves from our ingrained self-centeredness, which means we also have to work on ourselves, on our own minds, with some seriousness. Compassion isn't just about others. It's also about ourselves. We have to go deeper than the usual viewpoint of self versus others. It isn't enough to be polite or know the right ways to talk to people. We have to have a change of heart. With this change of heart comes resilience.

At this point the logic of our training program becomes clear. It starts with resolve and motivation: you have to know what you're doing and why, and based on these reflections, you firmly decide to take up the training. In this case, you realize that it's time to get serious about your life and that being serious means getting over your old habit of self-obsession, which in turn means developing genuine empathy and compassion. Reflecting on all of this at some depth, you **Resolve to begin** (point one).

Next, although you might not be quite ready for it and might have to go back to it later, likely more than once, you contemplate at some depth the nature of self and other, which gives you a conceptual understanding as well as an experiential handle on what it would really mean to fully embrace compassion. You see (and this may be a sobering vision) that to authentically receive others, you also have to be willing to deal with pain—yours as well as theirs (point two, **Train in empathy and compassion**).

This gets your attention and puts you on notice that the training you have undertaken is thorough and profound. It's not a walk in the park. Now it becomes obvious that it is crucially important to be ready for difficulties, because difficulties are sure to arise, and if they discourage you and you don't know how to endure them and make use of them, then all the work you've done so far will blow away in the wind (point three, **Transform bad circumstances into the path**).

Having worked on that—at least to the point of questioning your usual impulse to run away from or eliminate difficulties—your level of commitment and seriousness increases until there's no difference between your mind training and your life. The discipline no longer feels like something extra added on top of what you normally do, another item on your to-do list. You are practicing all the time, even when it feels like you're not (point four, **Make practice your whole life**).

Next you learn how to assess and regulate your practice with some subtlety, so you can encourage yourself to stay on the path and avoid veering off this way or that way. You recognize the subtle inner signs of your distraction and avoidance and learn to dance with them rather than losing track of yourself because of them (point five, **Assess and extend**).

Notice that most of this is about working with your own mind. Although we've considered compassion on a profound, an almost abstract, level, the slogans have yet to instruct us in the down and dirty daily struggles that we are having with the people in our lives. Now is the time for that: point six, **The discipline of relationship.**

Simply contemplating the wording of this point gives us pause. **The *discipline* of relationship?** We don't usually think of relationship as a discipline. But it is a discipline after all. For it is through relationship that we most fruitfully expand our horizons and train our minds to be compassionate and resilient.

We learn how to be human through our interaction with others. This process began at the beginning, when we were infants learning language and basic human responses from our mothers, and it has continued ever since. Such interaction is rich and full of possibility; it is a tremendous challenge and a tremendous opportunity.

We need others so much, and yet nothing is more troublesome than others. As Sartre said in his play *No Exit,* "Hell is other people." From spousal to international relations, people-to-people exchanges seem so difficult, nearly impossible. With all the wounding that has gone on so far, all the misunderstanding and confusion, getting along with others is very complicated, and the better we know others, the closer to them we are and the more dealings we have with them, the harder it gets. We might consider ourselves to be kind and reasonable people, but others seem not to be so reasonable. Or maybe we are not so kind and reasonable: maybe we have a hard time figuring out what we want and how to act toward others. Since they are the same way, dealing with ourselves and them at the same time is daunting indeed.

I have made something of a study of this question in my years of working with conflict-resolution professionals in partnership with the Center for Understanding in Conflict, a group of wise lawyers and mediators who have been working with the question of conflict in human interaction for more than thirty years. I have learned from them that conflict is not the exception in human relations—it is the rule. Its roots are deep, common, and various, and not easy to deal with, and there is no substitute for simply wading out into the deep waters of conflict with honesty, fierceness, and a willingness to plunge into the depth of human feeling when necessary. Regardless of how calm, good, and nice we think we have become, as long as we and others have desires and needs, we will clash, and if we don't expect this and learn how to deal with it, we will either have to live in some sequestered self-protective way or be embroiled in stressful controversy much of the time. Human relationship is indeed a discipline, and a complicated one at that. Yet how could we ever develop altruism and compassion, and therefore some measure of personal happiness, connection, and wisdom, if we can't get down to basics and deal with people as they actually are, in the world as it actually is, with all of its messiness? All of our training so far must lead us finally to this point. Now it's time to practice directly within the crazy human world.

But, again, remember: dealing with others isn't just dealing with others. We think of it that way, but that's a mistake. Dealing with others is dealing with ourselves dealing with others. There are no others apart from us, and there is no us apart from them. Our problems with others are our problems with ourselves and vice versa. Recognizing this is the first principle. Practicing the discipline of relationship is exactly training ourselves to understand and act in relation to others in ways we are not used to acting. That's what the slogans under this point do: they train us to take ourselves in hand so that we can be different in our interactions with others. Gradually we learn that when we are different, others are different too, because without our understanding that we have been doing this, we have been cocreating with others the conflicts and interpersonal hassles of our lives.

And since this is so problematic, we need a lot of guidance, many slogans, many suggestions. There are sixteen slogans under this point, some of them surprising and quite drastic:

23. **Come back to basics.**
24. **Don't be a phony.**
25. **Don't talk about faults.**
26. **Don't figure others out.**
27. **Work with your biggest problems first.**
28. **Abandon hope.**
29. **Don't poison yourself.**
30. **Don't be so predictable.**
31. **Don't malign others.**
32. **Don't wait in ambush.**
33. **Don't make everything so painful.**
34. **Don't unload on everyone.**
35. **Don't go so fast.**
36. **Don't be tricky.**
37. **Don't make gods into demons.**
38. **Don't rejoice at others' pain.**

**Come back to basics.**

In order to embark on the difficult voyage that the discipline of relationship turns out to be, we have to pause for a moment and return to basics. It might be a good idea at this point to go all the way back to the beginning, to the four reflections that we considered under the first slogan, **Train in the preliminaries:**

*The rarity and preciousness of human life.*
*The absolute inevitability of death.*

*The awesome and indelible power of our actions.*
*The inescapability of suffering.*

You might even want to pause and reread those pages.

When you keep in mind that your human life and the lives of others are rare and precious, that you and everyone else has to die someday, that no one escapes suffering, and that all of your words and deeds, and even thoughts and feeling, have big impacts on the world—when that is part of what you are aware of when you are aware of conflict with others, things change somewhat. These reflections may take the edge off your hurt or aggression and reframe for you what you are dealing with.

Recall your original intention to take up mind training. Recall the firmness of your decision to do so. Nothing is more common than the person who does spiritual practice for a long time with great commitment and intensity but completely forgets about it as soon as he or she gets singed by the heat of human relationship. Somehow we consider spirituality to be a private, personal matter. As important as we may think we think it is, actually we don't really think of it as being real or important. Since our spiritual practice is private and just for us, and since we don't have that much sense of our own reality (though, at the same time, we are self-obsessed: the two go together), we actually consider spiritual practice a kind of self-indulgent luxury. This is why as soon as we are embroiled in a problem with someone else, our good spiritual intentions tend to dissolve. As soon as our lives get powerfully drawn into the lives of others, as soon as those others awaken our desire, our rage, our shame, or our fear, we immediately lose track of what we are doing, compelled by the seemingly greater reality of the presence of another in our life. There's no distraction like a human relationship. So it makes sense to renew our commitment at this point, so that we can turn the distraction of relationship into the discipline of relationship, the spiritual practice of relationship.

In the commentarial tradition, **Come back to basics** comprises three points. The first point is more or less what I've just said, *Renew and keep to your commitments.* The second point is *Don't act outrageously.* In ancient India and Tibet, this meant things like don't chop down trees where spirits dwell, don't pee in rivers, don't hug lepers. That is, refrain from dangerous, antisocial, or attention-grabbing activities, outrageous things that would draw attention to you. This may seem an odd thing to bring up in this context, but maybe not. Possibly up to now we have been tempted a time or two to be a bit precious or overearnest about our spiritual endeavors. We may have felt a bit holier-than-thou more than once. This is no good in any case, but perhaps not so bad in the privacy of your own mind. But now that we are about to embark on the practice of interacting with others, it becomes really bad to come off as though we were holy and spiritual. As if somehow because of the virtue of our commitments and spiritual efforts, we are conducting ourselves differently from the general run of humanity. Clearly this would be a huge problem for our relationships. Nothing makes people feel criticized and even a little hostile like someone else's pretentious efforts to be good. So, *Don't act outrageously.* Keep your efforts to practice the discipline of human relationship within the bounds of ordinary human interaction. Don't appear to be different from anyone else. One way or another, we're all in this game together.

The third point is *Don't be one-sided.* This one is very important in human relations, and it runs exactly counter to the usual way we approach things. Usually we are exactly one-sided: there's our side and the other person's side, and it's our side that is important, correct, or right, so much so that we may not even notice that there is another side. But there's always another side. This may be so, but that also may be so. This may be so today, but tomorrow it may not be so. If there's a side, there's always another side.

*Don't be one-sided* has another sense too—don't favor people you like over people you don't like. Try not to be one-sided in that way. This seems impossible and inadvisable. Are we really supposed to regard an acquaintance or an enemy the same way we regard our close friends, our spouse, and our children? Realistically, no. But that's not the point. The point is to notice how much in almost all of our encounters we are subtly preju diced by our one-sidedness, constantly upholding ourselves and those we like and running down (in however small a way) those we don't like. These prejudices, which we take for granted and affirm, actually cause us more trouble than we realize. They create a subtle climate of preference, for and against, that gives rise to more of our interpersonal rough spots than we realize. So even though we may not be able to have equal feelings toward all, this slogan puts us on notice that we better take our one-sidedness into account and do what we can to deemphasize it.

**Don't be a phony.**

As I've already noted, it is tempting to think that if we seriously take up spiritual practice, we're going to be different from the ordinary run of people. We're going to be spiritual people, not like those unspiritual others. So naturally we feel different and act differently. We're very kind but maybe a little stiff, a little too deliberate about everything we do, very mindful about everything.

This is typical. If you go to a monastery, you'll notice that the newer monastics are like this. Certainly it was like this in the Zen center where I lived for many years. The newer residents were very careful with the Zen forms, very precise, very polite, perfect, and stiff.

This slogan's point is clear: If you're going to revolutionize your life, please do. But don't impose some sort of regimen on yourself. **Don't be a phony.** In fact, as you go on, you begin to see that the spiritual process is exactly the opposite of this: that you've been imposing a regimen on yourself all of your life, you took it to be yourself—and now finally you can stop, you can relax, you don't have to impress anyone, especially yourself.

So when you notice you're imposing something on yourself, when your efforts to be good and practice slogans begin to feel like you're wearing a straitjacket, then I have a slogan for you: "Lighten up, relax, maybe go to a movie, have a glass of wine, don't try so hard, maybe there's something good on TV."

**Don't talk about faults.**

If you were to practice this slogan as an absolute, literal rule, it would do wonders for your relationships. Imagine never, under any circumstances, discussing the faults of others. Try it for a week. You will probably discover with some shock how much of what you say (and hear) involves in one way or another discussing the faults of others. But if you could actually refrain from this kind of speech entirely, you would become an unusually likeable person. Others, without knowing why, would be drawn to you. This is because it is completely normal for people to speak critically, even disparagingly, of one another. Even friends do it to and about friends. But although we all enjoy this sort of seemingly innocent gossip, it also makes us nervous. What are the others saying about *us* when we are not around? This makes us wary of one another, and this wariness is so normal that we don't even think of it as wariness. So the person who doesn't do this, who seems to be consistently supportive and forgiving, stands out.

But the obvious problem is, what do you do when others actually are at fault—which happens quite a lot—or when to opt out of discussions of the faults of others would be so socially awkward as to be nearly impossible? What do you do then? Ignore the conversation or the fault, deny it, or pretend it's not a fault? What about when that's untenable?

The fact is, when someone is acting badly, is being nasty or obnoxious or corrupt or cruel, or even just plain stupid or incompetent, your speaking of that person's faults in a harsh or critical way, however deserving of such speech the person may be, doesn't help. It generally makes a bad situation worse. This is so whether you speak to the person directly or snipe behind his or her back, and the person eventually discovers this or senses it from the responses of others. The effect of such criticism is generally that the person gets upset, feels attacked, which inspires him or her to continue on in the same vein. The traditional wording of this slogan is *Don't speak of injured limbs*. The concept is that everyone who acts or speaks destructively or foolishly or even incompetently is like a person with an injured limb. If you see someone with a deformed hip or with stumps for arms, the injury is obvious. And just as we don't criticize someone for having an injury like that, although we recognize it as an injury and note the limitations that come from it, we aren't critical of the person with an inner injury that is the ultimate cause of the person's poor conduct. In just the same way, we can recognize the injury and the limitations that it engenders and respect them.

You can always count on the fact that people who behave badly have been injured. If you need to correct them, you can do so with that in mind. With some sympathy. Such people need to figure out how to heal their wounds someday, and very likely your speaking to them or about them harshly and with disrespect will not bring that about. It won't inspire them, you, or other listeners. In fact, the opposite is probably the case: speaking to or about a wounded, nasty person with kindness and warmth—when the person has been conditioned by almost all of his or her relationships to expect the opposite—may indeed cause surprising transformation. But this is hard, if not impossible, to do if you don't really see and appreciate the injury in the first place. If you see only the fault and not the injury. So practicing **Don't talk about faults** would involve noticing when you are doing this, remembering that there's an injury behind every fault, softening, and then maybe conditioning yourself, little by little, to speak differently.

### Don't figure others out.

Who could ever understand another person? Even a cursory investigation (which just a little meditation practice will provide) shows us that we barely understand ourselves. There is so much going on in our mind if we will only stop to look at it, all sorts of contradictory and underappreciated phenomena. If it's hard to fathom ourselves, how could we seriously believe we can figure out someone else? Yet think of all the time we spend analyzing and discussing our friends and relatives, as if we knew what was going on with them, as if we had a real line on them and their problems. Who can fathom why people do what they do? Who can fathom what makes another person tick? Jack Himmelstein, of the Center for Understanding in Conflict, has a very wise saying about this: "We judge ourselves by our intentions; we judge others by the effects of their actions on us." This is one reason we so often come out on the righteous side of our conflicts: we know (or think we know) our own inmost intentions; we assume the intentions of others based on our understanding of their outward acts. And we are usually wrong.

This slogan says, give up this strategy. When you find yourself thinking about someone else's motives, needs, or feelings, catch yourself and recognize that your thoughts and perceptions are probably quite wide of the mark. Catch yourself in midthought and remember that you don't really know what someone else is thinking or feeling. Ignorant, you are better off assuming that everyone is doing his or her best and that everyone is on the same human journey you are on. Maybe at the moment another person's journey is not going so well, maybe at the moment it is leading him or her down some nasty dark alleyways. But who knows the way a person is supposed to go? The person may have to go down a dark alley first to come out into the light later, and that's just how it is for him or her.

We try our best to be supportive of our friends, and that's good. Sometimes they seek out our advice and we give it, and that's good too. But in the end probably the best thing we could do for them—or for anyone—is to let them alone, profoundly alone, in the recognition that they are so much more than we could ever understand. Leaving them alone doesn't mean abandoning them or not loving them. It means recognizing their full human dignity. Practicing **Don't figure others out** is training our minds to recall, even in the midst of controversy with others, that we don't really know what is in another's heart and that whatever we imagine is probably incorrect. To be sure, there are times when it may be a good idea to try to imagine what someone else is feeling, thinking, needing, or wanting. (Remember, the slogans can't be applied like blunt instruments: they require the wisdom of flexibility.) But when we do that, in the light of this slogan, we do it with humility, knowing that we may be mistaken.

### Work with your biggest problems first.

Each one of us is given our own personal gift of craziness, our own preferred tendency for decompensation. Some get angry, some depressed, some anxious. Some are meddlesome, some lazy, some hyperactive, some distractible. One of the insights of mind training (and it comes as a great relief) is that there is no normal. We are all abnormal, each in our own delightful way. The trick is, first, to accept this, and next, to have some idea of the most important ways in which you are abnormal. Let's say it's anger. You anger easily, and when you are angry you are miserable, and you inevitably say and do stupid things for which you later feel remorse and shame—and you've been this way all of your life. So good, now you are aware of your personal gift, your treasure. I have already mentioned Suzuki Roshi's crucial saying, "For a Zen student, a weed is a treasure." Rather than seeing your problem with anger as a personal defect to be hidden or overcome, you see this weed as a treasure. You don't resolve to work on other things and save this most difficult one for later. You resolve to pay attention to it now and keep on paying attention until, through your continued attention over time, things begin to change. Later, something else will be your biggest problem. It's always something. Working with this slogan helps you to see that you don't need to overcome your biggest problems overnight, nor should you defer them to another time. Pay attention right now to what bothers you the most about yourself in your relationships to others and trust that simply by paying attention, little by little you will see what you need to do.

**Abandon hope.**

**Abandon hope?** This slogan seems shocking at first. Surely hope is a good thing. Doesn't hope lie at the center of the whole proposition of mind training? Probably you do have some hope that mind training will have a positive impact on your life, that it will help you to improve as a human being, that you'll be wiser, kinder, more connected to others as a result of the training. Very possibly some of what I've written so far in this book has given you reason to have such hopes.

Hopefulness is no doubt preferable to hopelessness or apathy.

But there's a downside to hope. If we hope that mind training is going to do this or that for us, and if we measure our progress and become crestfallen when progress does not match the image our hope has projected, then hope becomes counterproductive. Hope easily becomes discouragement. In this sense, hope is limiting and unhelpful. So this slogan takes a drastic stance, a bracing shot of ice water in the face: **Abandon hope.**

Let's think more closely about how hope for personal improvement actually works. Life is very mysterious. The closer we get to ourselves and to our actual intimate experience, the more mysterious it seems. As we learn, especially on our meditation cushions (but it is true all the time), life unfolds in a profoundly immediate and continuous present. Somehow the moment of the immediate past gets swallowed up in time and completely disappears as each moment gives way to a new moment. The past is constantly going and gone, and the new present is similar to but never exactly the same as the immediate past—and this goes on moment after moment. This means that no matter what we do or don't do, we're going to change, and we always have been changing. So we don't need to hope for change. There will be change, and there always has been change.

On the other hand, do we actually change? It seems that we don't. Inside, we probably all feel pretty much the same as we felt when we were ten years old: our basic feeling of subjectivity, of being ourselves, is exactly the same, despite all the surface changes it seems we have undergone, decade by decade, year by year, moment by moment.

So: on one hand, change is every minute. On the other hand, there is no change. The French say, "The more things change, the more they remain the same."

So what change are we hoping for?

But of course, conventionally, our character does change over time, we all know that. And the question is, are we improving or getting worse? And how would we know? If today, let's say, you are a mixed-up, unhappy person who wants to improve, you probably have an idea about what that improvement would look or feel like, however undeveloped that idea might be. This means that from the standpoint of confusion and unhappiness, you're imagining an improved you. How could that vision of an improved you not be distorted in some serious way, since it is the projection of a confused and unhappy person? Could it be that that distorted vision of an improved you is not only inherently unattainable but, worse, potentially sabotaging? Given this, all of your senses of what it means to improve or to fail to improve would necessarily be off base, and your hope for improvement would therefore be entirely counterproductive. Is it ever possible, from one position, to imagine what it's like in another position? Of course we do this all the time, but it's never accurate. My thought of what it is going to be like when I arrive in Mexico is never the same as what it is actually like when I arrive in Mexico, even though I have been to Mexico many times and know what to expect. The concrete, visceral reality of the present is never the same as what we imagined, in the present, of the future.

I've been doing Zen practice for a long time, so when people are considering taking up the practice, they are likely to ask me what I've gained from it. How has my life changed? I always say, yes of course I am much different now from who I was forty years ago. But then again, when forty years goes by, anyone is different, Zen practice or no. How can I tell how much the differences of forty years have to do with my Zen practice? Who knows whether the changes that have occurred in my life are the consequences simply of forty years of life on earth among others?

That's one problem. Another problem is: have the various changes been an improvement? Well, yes. I think I am more stable, more ethical, more empathic; maybe I am a little wiser, calmer; maybe I have a better sense of what my life is about than I did before. But also, no: in forty years' time many things have gotten worse. Forty years ago I was younger; I had more physical endurance, more strength, a better memory, I was smarter, I could meditate better; I had more buoyancy. Improvement? Hard to say.

**Abandon hope.** That is, don't look for or celebrate improvement, and don't imagine there is no improvement or that you are getting worse. Since it really is impossible to say for certain whether or not we have improved, it is better not to frustrate ourselves with such useless questions and instead to keep on going with the training in the faith that it is worthwhile for its own sake. This faith isn't religious faith in the usual sense—a leap of faith in Buddha or Buddhism or meditation practice. It is faith we find through our own experience over the time of our training. Somehow, as we continue, we come to the definite feeling that this training is simply the right thing to do. We know it. We don't have to convince ourselves or anyone else. We don't need evidence. We simply feel the rightness of the training in the middle of our lives. We are quite happy to do our best to maintain a joyful mind as we go on practicing right now. That becomes enough.

Despite what I've just said about the impossibility, the uselessness, and even the counterproductivity of our actually knowing whether or not we are improving, the truth is many people who do the practice see all kinds of wonderful improvements in their lives. I am always quite cheered up when they tell me about it. But I have noticed that the sense of big improvement comes mostly at the beginning, in the first years (or decades). As you keep on going, you hardly notice improvements anymore. Improvements may be there, and others might appreciate them, but you yourself simply stop noticing particularly. For you, practice disappears as a vehicle for self-improvement, and the only thing important for you now is to live your life, which means to continue your mind training. Shunryu Suzuki called this "practice without a gaining idea."

So this slogan is telling you: when you are excited about your progress or discouraged about your lack of progress, let go of that silly thought. **Abandon all hope** and go happily on.

### Don't poison yourself.

The slogan **Don't poison yourself** is a corollary to **Abandon hope.** The poison referred to is the poison of self-centeredness, which is always so sneaky. Remember, the point of all of our training is to reduce our self-worry and self-concern and be worried and concerned for others. So **Stop poisoning yourself** with self-concern. When you notice instances of self-criticism, discouragement, or pride, remember this slogan. It's fine that those things come up. Of course they will; it is natural. Your goal is not to eliminate them but rather to practice this slogan. To know what these attitudes are and to stop eating them and poisoning yourself with them. Instead, "No, thank you, I don't eat that stuff anymore; I know it's bad for me."

### Don't be so predictable.

If, as we've just been saying, you and everyone else you know are unfathomable, then why do you persist in imagining that you know who you and everyone else are and, based on these fixed ideas, that you can predict your behavior and that of others? Freshness and openness and a capacity for surprise are hallmarks of mind training, which is one reason why it is so much fun. It is not, as it might seem to us (mapping onto it our received sense of morality or upright conduct), a matter of being ethical and sober in all of our actions. It is very much the opposite: we view with bemused curiosity our various responses and habits, even when it is clear that they are not too wholesome or even sane. With mind training we are quite honest about what is going on, never pretending, never whitewashing or denying, but at the same time not assuming that we have to give in to or believe our every impulse and thought. We are all quite predictable because we are all fixated on identities we have constructed (with the help of our families and friends) that we consider to be accurate reflections of our possibilities. But they are not. Yes, maybe you are an angry person, and you can't help but notice that anger arises in you frequently when certain sorts of events trigger it. But, anger having arisen, what now do you do with it? **Don't be so predictable!** There are many possibilities. I have never been angry in this moment before, so why would I want to project onto this moment all of my past moments of having been angry? To quote again our beloved Zen teacher Shunryu Suzuki, "In the beginner's mind there are many possibilities, in the expert's mind few." **Don't be so predictable** is telling us to cultivate beginner's mind in relation to ourselves and our own experiences. To stop being such experts on ourselves. We should all stop becoming professional selves and become amateur selves. An amateur is someone who does what he does for the love of it, not for advancement or money. Imagine being yourself for the love of discovering every day who you are in relation to others: loving them, and yourself in the process of loving them. In this sense we are all a bit too professional about our lives and our relationships, engaging in them for self-advantage, which reduces the love—and the fun. Amateurs always have more fun than professionals. Professionals have to be predictable; amateurs can't be.

**Don't malign others.**

The slogan **Don't malign others,** like many others in this sixth point, is nothing fancy. It is just good common sense, common in all cultures in all times the world over. It's advice you might have gotten from your mother. In fact, I actually did get this advice from my mother when I was a boy, and it worked like magic.

When I was in the sixth grade, going into the seventh grade, I changed schools. I was leaving all the friends I had known and the familiar school and going to a much larger school in another town. This was a very frightening experience for me, because I had never been out of the little town that I grew up in. I was convinced that all the children in the new school would be much smarter and much more sophisticated than I was, probably also taller and older than I. Maybe I would get very poor grades, maybe nobody would like me, I wouldn't have any friends. I was really worried about this all summer before school began. I went to my mother and said: "What am I going to do? What can I do?" And she said, "Don't worry about anything, just don't make nasty remarks about others and everything will turn out okay." So I took this advice to heart, and I resolved I would never make a single nasty remark about anyone, ever.

I can vividly remember the moment that I was standing in a group of children who were all making nasty remarks about somebody. I became really frightened, because it was expected that I would also make such remarks, and now what was I going to do? But I didn't say anything. Everyone else was talking, but I literally didn't say a word, and the rest of the school year I never made a single nasty remark about anybody. Motivated by my fear, I had a strong determination to practice this slogan. In my mind, it was a matter of survival. I didn't understand why this would help, but I trusted my mother, so I did exactly what she said. By the end of the school year, to my great astonishment, I realized that people liked me and were saying nice things about me. This really surprised me; I couldn't figure out how that had happened. And then I realized it was because my mother was right, that if you don't make nasty remarks about people, people will like you. Since then I have kept this practice, and it has been one of the greatest practices of a lifetime for me. Because of it, I get to tell this story about my mother from time to time, which I am sure is making her very happy, wherever she is.

### Don't wait in ambush.

**Don't wait in ambush** means don't hold a grudge. If someone says or does something hurtful to you, don't hold it inside, nursing it and keeping watch, waiting for that moment when you can leap out of the bushes and attack the person that did this to you. All the time that you were lurking there in the bushes, you were losing yourself without realizing it, losing your practice, losing the opportunity to learn from your pain and hurt and open up. Instead you were lurking in hiding, festering your hurt, making it bigger and more virulent. This slogan is simply saying that when you find yourself lurking behind a bush or a tree, come out into the open. Don't look for revenge. If you have an enemy, try to engage the enemy with energy and compassion, straightforwardly; don't be sneaky and hide behind a rock. Learn to identify what it feels like inside to be lurking, become aware of the sorts of thoughts and feelings that arise when you are lurking, because often we are lurking and we don't know we're lurking. Once you begin to know that you are lurking when you are lurking, commit yourself to coming out from behind the bush or tree into the open, where you can feel what you are feeling and express yourself as best you can.

### Don't make everything so painful.

In Zen we have a colorful way of making the point **Don't make everything so painful:** "Don't put a head on top of your head." In other words, if something is bad, it's bad; don't make it worse. This slogan is specifically about dealing with others. If someone is a difficult, troublesome person, don't make the person worse. Don't elaborate the person's many faults, and don't begin acting toward him or her in such a way that those very faults will become even more severe. The opposite idea is much better: without expecting someone to be any better than he or she is, act toward the person in a way that would minimize rather than maximize the problems.

It usually happens this way: someone is nasty or difficult because, as we have just contemplated, she has an injured limb. Naturally she is going to act like someone with an injured limb, and this is going to cause almost everyone to look at her and say, "You're a really terrible person." Usually we won't say this to the person directly, we'll say it to one another, and even then it might not be direct, it may be subtle, in jokes or offhanded remarks. But even if the person never directly hears what others think of her, she will surely get the message strongly enough, in looks and gestures, in remarks, because there is no way for a person not to know what others are feeling about her. Now the injured person recognizes, "Oh, look at the way everyone treats me. I guess I really am a terrible person. People don't like me. Well, if I am that way, if people are going to treat me that way, then I will show them something. You thought that was bad so far? How about this!" In this way the person's bad behavior and bad self-view becomes reinforced, keeps building on itself, and what was bad to begin with becomes worse and worse. Probably this is how very injured people become inspired to buy firearms and go into their workplaces and schools and shoot their coworkers.

The way we treat injured people is very natural and logical, but the logic is essentially faulty. Instead of noting that a terrible person is terrible and, based on this, treating him as if he were terrible, it would be much better to treat the person with tremendous kindness exactly because he is so terrible. Doesn't this make more sense? We think it is natural, and emotionally true, to be kind and sweet to people who are kind and sweet and to be terrible to terrible people. But it should be just the opposite. If we have to be denigrating and mean, it is better to be denigrating and mean to kind, sweet people, because it probably won't bother them so much; or if it does bother them, it won't ruin them completely, because they are already kind and nice, and although they may be somewhat hurt by our disrespect, it probably won't ruin their character. If we are kind and sweet to someone who is terrible and who, because of being terrible, is conditioned to being treated that way, our kindness might change him, it might surprise him, it might even shock him into better behavior.

And what about when we take the process I am describing here and turn it on ourselves: believing we are terrible people, we treat ourselves like terrible people and become more and more terrible as a result. **Don't make everything so painful.** When things are painful with other people or within your own mind, try to identify the actual pain and the actual problem. Then focus on that. Try not to elaborate on it with too much complaining or a proliferation of thinking or words and deeds that will make it worse. Don't put a head on top of your head. One head is enough.

### Don't unload on everyone.

The traditional slogan reads *Don't put an ox's load on a cow.* This gives you a picture of life in ancient India or Tibet, as do some of the other slogans. You can imagine people hiding behind bushes and waiting to ambush each other, people eating poisonous food or trying to serve poisonous food to their enemies, people cutting down trees with evil tree spirits in them or peeing in sacred streams, and, as here, people in their villages with their oxen and their cows. Oxen are sturdy animals. They pull heavy burdens, they're made for that. Cows, on the other hand, give milk. They are not built for carrying heavy burdens. So don't put an ox's burden on a cow. The idea is: you are the ox, other people are the cow. The burden of your suffering is your own; not theirs. So don't unload on them; don't try to give your burden to them.

This goes deeper than our merely forbearing from dumping all of our emotion on other people. And certainly it is not saying that we should keep our suffering to ourselves. Sharing our stories of suffering with one another is one of the most important ways we have of connecting to one another. We have to do that, and we have to learn how and when to do it. So this slogan is not telling us to clam up, to keep our sorrows to ourselves. Instead, this is a slogan about karma, or causality, about how all of us are responsible for our own deeds.

Suppose someone does some really bad things to you; she may oppress you a great deal, treat you unfairly, and so on. This is really bad, and one way or the other the person is going to have to bear the burden of what she has done. In other words, in relation to these misdeeds of hers, she is the ox. But in relation to you, she is the cow—the suffering that you are feeling as a result of her deeds is not her burden, it is yours, though her deeds have caused you to feel the suffering. After all, if someone were to abuse you, and somehow or other you were able to gobble up the abuse and deal with it cheerfully and make your practice stronger, so that by the time he was finished abusing you, you were happier and stronger than you had ever been before, then his abuse wouldn't have hurt you, it would have helped you. It wouldn't have been a cause of your suffering, it would have been a cause of your joy. The reason the abuse is so painful is because of the way you have reacted to it. If you're not there when an attacker is hitting you on the head, or if you don't have a head, the attacker is just hitting air or some other object. It's because you are there and because you do have a head that the harm is happening. I realize this is odd reasoning, but it's true. All suffering is your own burden, an ox's burden. Ultimately the burden of your suffering is you own, you yourself are the immediate cause of it, even though the occasion may have been someone else's misdeed.

So, although we might suffer at the hands of others, if we blame others for our suffering, if we try to put the burden of our suffering on them, it doesn't do a thing to them, but it increases our own burden, because now we have become the victim of others, which means now we are completely dependent on them to relieve our suffering and now we are pleading and begging with them to relieve our suffering. They must be punished or they must make amends or apologize, and if none of this happens, we are going to continue to suffer. But the truth is that only we can bear the burden of our own suffering. If we take responsibility for the suffering, then we have the power to lift that burden off even if the other person continues to abuse us and is never punished and never makes amends.

In other words, somebody can put us in jail, but the only one who can take away our freedom is ourselves, and likewise the only one who can give us our freedom is ourselves. When we give our responsibility for our suffering to others, we are giving up our power to overcome the suffering.

To be sure, this is a spiritual teaching, not a legal or a political one. To ensure social justice, wrongdoers have to be tried and punished and victims compensated. None of that is in contradiction to this slogan. The job of the law and of society is to promote and secure justice and to write and uphold laws that will have that effect. But spiritually, it is for each of us our own responsibility to shoulder the burden of our own suffering, whatever its cause, and to turn the burden into wisdom and love. Sometimes this spiritual reality, when not appreciated, can spill over into law or politics. When a society or a culture doesn't promote or validate this spiritual truth and instead encourages its citizens to blame others for their suffering rather than take spiritual responsibility for it themselves, there can be very toxic social dynamics, like racism or xenophobia or unjust and ungenerous economic social policies. "Why should we help them," the argument goes, "when it is their laziness or lack of ambition that is bankrupting *us*?"

### Don't go so fast.

Mind training is not a race to a finish line. It is not a task we are performing and the faster we perform it the faster we can go on to other things. As we have already established, mind training is the practice of a lifetime—our lifetime will end soon enough, there is certainly no rush to bring that eventuality about. Nor are we doing mind training in competition with someone else, so that we are motivated to speed up the process to accomplish more in less time than the other person does. **Don't go so fast** is an invitation to notice our impatience, our silly fixation on perfection and accomplishment, and when we do, to have a good laugh with ourselves and drop it. Literally to stop, take a breath, and let go.

Becoming a grown-up, fully developed, wise, and kind human being is a long, slow process. Collectively, we began this process a long time ago; it continues throughout our lifetime and goes on after that, as others continue the journey. It is a large and noble undertaking. There is no point in hurrying it, and there is no way to hurry it anyway. It really makes no difference how far you get in your lifetime, because no matter how far you get, there will always be further to go. And the very act of measurement or evaluation is a misunderstanding of the nature of the process.

### Don't be tricky.

Basic, clear, and guileless motivation is everything in mind training. With meditation practice, which inspires basic mindfulness all the time, which in turn promotes a willing, cheerful self-honesty, we can continually check our motivation. **Don't be tricky** is useful in that endeavor. We are trying to cultivate altruism deeply and seriously, and our motivation for doing this comes not from a desire to win friends and influence people (though it is wonderful to have friends, and if we can influence people for the good, this is worthwhile) but from our conviction, based on long reflection, that the cultivation of altruism is simply the best, truest, and most satisfying way to live. Mind training is not a sneaky, tricky way of networking or getting more clients or better dates. Nor is it a way for us to be known far and wide as a wonderful spiritual person, so that our friends will be admiring or envious and our enemies will be chagrined.

No doubt you have noticed people who are very, very nice and very, very sweet and very, very spiritual, but they make you very, very suspicious because you know they're trying to get something out of it—maybe even get something from you. You wonder what their angle is. Of course *you* are not like that; only others can be like that. When you notice that you are very frequently encountering others who are like that, it is probably a good idea to look more closely at yourself and see whether, in fact, in some subtle way you, too, are trying to gain all sorts of advantages and points by being a nice person others will admire. Probably you do have this motivation, at least in part. We all do. There may not be any such thing as pure innocent motivation. **Don't be tricky** is a device to help us to notice this and be real about it. Not be bothered by it, and not be fooled by it either. We train because we know it's the best way to live, not to get our way, become rich, make people like us, or prove to our brother-in-law that he really is a nasty person, because next to you who are so kind and so good and so sweet, he looks really bad.

In this wide world you can find many people who think that meditation and spiritual practice are really stupid. Who has time for such stuff, they may feel, and even if there were time, isn't spiritual practice a bunch of hooey anyway, the province of the pious or naive, laughable in its transparent foolishness? I think most people look at it that way.

But there are a lot of people who think it's wonderful and admirable to seriously take up a spiritual path and who wish they had the time and the discipline to do it, people who will admire you if you meditate, do yoga, if you are wise and healthy and a vegetarian or even a vegan. So in certain circles we can be quite proud of our spiritual efforts, and we can get a lot of credit for them. "Oh, yes, I've been meditating every day for many years, many years; I'm a vegetarian." When we are finally able to peek through our self-satisfaction and self-deception and notice the pride we have been generating in ourselves for our fine spiritual efforts, we should simply admit it, be able to laugh at ourselves, and forgive ourselves. Selfish motivation is perfectly normal, and we will always be dealing with it.

We can appreciate this slogan more and more as we continue. As with all the slogans, "don't do this" or "don't do that" doesn't mean don't do this or that, because we can't really prevent something like self-deception ("trickiness") from arising in our hearts. What the slogan means is take an honest and lighthearted look at yourself and be ready to forgive yourself for your natural foibles. And always be ready to go forward without regret or self-blame.

**Don't make gods into demons.**

Gods dwell in heavenly realms, pleasant places, and demons dwell in horrible, nasty hell realms. This slogan is telling us not to make the pleasant things in our lives into burning hells because of dissatisfaction and complaining. Not to demand so much of ourselves and our circumstances or so much of others that we lose sight of the positive circumstances that may apply in our lives. When you try to be perfect, or even to be good, you usually come up short. Grousing about this, you may fail to notice how well you have been doing and how fortunate your circumstances are. All you can see are problems.

Here's a story we always told at the Zen Hospice Project, where I worked and taught for many years: One of our clients was a man in a really miserable situation—he was all alone, he had no family, he was in pain, he was bedridden, he had accomplished very little in his life, and now he was dying. If he had wanted to construct a hell for himself, he certainly had plenty of materials to work with. And yet he didn't do this. Far from turning gods into demons, he seemed to turn demons into gods. He found things to appreciate, even in the middle of his dire situation. Although he had plenty to complain about, he seldom complained. Instead he praised: he praised the view outside his window on sunny days, when flowers were in bloom; he praised the sponge baths the attendants gave him; and above all, he praised the cool, clean sheets that he got into after the sponge baths. I always remember this because since then I have also made it a practice to notice how pleasant clean sheets are when you first get into them, especially after a shower or a bath.

I sometimes wonder how people in really bad situations, wars or famines or severe natural disasters, manage to survive. But I then reflect that no matter what is going on, there are always small moments in which we can find some joy or relief, if we are open to them. When there's a lot of pain in your body, you really do have something to complain about. But if you look closely, you will notice that pain isn't ever constant: it gets worse, it gets better, and sometimes it is even almost gone. I know this because I have experienced it personally, and more than once. If I can take joy in the moment of relief, when the pain subsides, I have a lot more patience for the pain when it comes back. If in the aftermath of an earthquake—even when your house has been knocked down—you can appreciate the warm bed relief workers have provided for you in the shelter and the beauty of the sky or a child's face, then you will have been victimized once, but not twice, by what has happened.

**Don't rejoice at others' pain.**

**Don't rejoice at others' pain** is the final slogan in point six, **The discipline of relationship**. This slogan is just what it sounds like: don't wish for something bad to happen to your enemy. Don't take delight in something bad that happens to someone you don't like (or someone you do like). Don't hope for someone to die so you can inherit money.

Even if there's a terrible leader who gets assassinated and this assassination brings in a much better government, don't dance at his funeral, don't rejoice; suffering is suffering, and it makes emotional sense to always feel compassion for suffering no matter who the sufferer is. Even if we can't forgive or condone the actions of our enemies, we don't need to wish misfortune on them or applaud when bad things befall them. It is important that those who do harm stop doing that and that we or someone, when possible, sees to it that that stopping occurs. But this isn't the same as revenge or enjoying another's pain. As we have seen, compassion, real compassion, can't be selective. Though we may not be able to avoid favoring those we love and feeling shaky about those who have hurt us, we are clear that compassion and empathy, if they are going to be of benefit at all, must be universally, not selectively, felt.

8

---

# Living with Ease
# in a Crazy World

PROBABLY BY NOW you've recognized that, as with all ancient systems of spiritual cultivation, the mind-training text has lots of repetition and overlap. Maybe the ancient pundits who devised this system weren't as organized or efficient as we are. Or maybe they deliberately included some redundancy, knowing that when it comes to mind training, you can't expect perfect efficiency and you're going to need to go over the same ground many times, in many ways. Perhaps they appreciated the nasty persistence of human folly—perhaps even nastier and more persistent the smarter and the more sophisticated we are.

I call this last point **Living with ease in a crazy world** because that's what this grab bag of final instructions is all about: how to take into account our own and the world's craziness and be able to live with it in grace and ease. In his commentary on mind training, the great twentieth-century Tibetan trickster-sage Chögyam Trungpa said that these last slogans were for the "post-meditation" stage. I've already discussed the Zen attitude toward "postmeditation" and most other distinctions, but let me extend those comments a bit here before we launch into a specific discussion of the final twenty-one slogans.

It seems that resistance to systems and distinctions is a big point for Zen. This entire text of mind training is for the purpose of reducing self-centeredness and generating compassion, yet in Zen it's said that there is no such thing as compassion, because reality is already compassionate by its very nature, so there's no such thing as compassion per se, as distinct from anything else. Why, then, prattle on about compassion? Nor is there any such thing as meditation, since consciousness is essentially meditation already. So why talk about meditation or postmeditation as distinct categories?

This is the humor, the Big Joke, of Zen practice that one finds over and over again in the sayings of the old masters. Whatever you privilege, whatever you define and adhere to, is always wrong and will, because wrong, always lead to a problem and a danger. Whether it is meditation or compassion or goodness or truth or enlightenment—whatever noble thing you'd want to know, experience, or aspire to—as soon as you privilege something and make a big deal out of it, there is always trouble. Whatever we designate as this or that, is just that, a designation, no more and no less, and we should recognize this and not get so excited about it.

Compassion, for instance, sounds like such a good idea, but the problem with it is that it will probably make us sentimental, softheaded, and overly enthusiastic, and this will tend to make us troublesome to exactly the people we want to have compassion for, because our excessive sentimentality and insistence on being helpful will probably be annoying and counterproductive. We will likely be tripping all over ourselves in our compassion, and in the process we will land with a thud on top of the very people we are trying to be compassionate toward. Also, quite possibly, our compassion will cause us to be disapproving or even hostile to others who we are certain are not as compassionate as we are. This, of course, is the opposite of compassion. Asked about what compassion really is, an old Zen master said, "It's like reaching back for your pillow in the dark." In other words, it's a simple and natural human act, no big deal.

And the trouble with meditation is that as soon as we identify something as meditation, we are likely to be precious about it. "Ah, yes, meditation, so peaceful, calm, focused." And then we sit down on our meditation cushion, and when we find that we are anything but peaceful, calm, and focused, we will be severely disapproving of ourselves, and in this way our precious meditation practice soon turns into a big stick with which we will hit ourselves over the head (no Zen master is required for this; we will do it quite well by ourselves). Of course, it could also go the other way. We could actually be peaceful, calm, and happy in our meditation and even in our lives—and therefore nervous about the prospect of losing that peace and calm and quite critical of all of those people and forces in the world that would seem to threaten our good state of mind. This is the trouble with the idea of meditation. Asked what meditation really is, "It's non-meditation," an old Zen master said. A monk then said to him, "How could meditation be nonmeditation?" The master replied, "It's alive!"

Therefore, our wise and practical Zen ancestors pointed out that there is nothing anywhere we can find to inflate ourselves with. It's not that self-inflation is a moral mistake; rather, it's a conceptual mistake, which in the end amounts to self-oppression and disparagement of others, both of which lead to great unhappiness for one's self. That's why Zen is so insistent on the Big Joke that reminds us that all designations are funny, funny in themselves, and even funnier (if tragically so) exactly because we take them so seriously. It is very obvious, if you actually look, that the emperor is naked and that we who keep imagining him clothed in finery are pretty foolish. This is why in Zen there's not much discussion about meditation or postmeditation or about compassion or lack of compassion. There is only everyday ordinary practice. The bell rings, "Oh, all right, meditation." The bell rings again, "Okay, get up, forget about meditation, it's gone." That's the spirit of Zen training. No sticking to anything. So, as I said in the beginning, we may need these slogans. Let's now contemplate these last twenty-one postmeditation slogans, making sure we keep their nakedness in mind.

39. **Keep a single intention.**
40. **Correct all wrongs with one intention.**
41. **Begin at the beginning, end at the end.**
42. **Be patient either way.**
43. **Observe, even if it costs you everything.**
44. **Train in three difficulties.**
45. **Take on the three causes.**
46. **Don't lose track.**
47. **Keep the three inseparable.**
48. **Train wholeheartedly, openly, and constantly.**
49. **Stay close to your resentment.**
50. **Don't be swayed by circumstances.**
51. **This time get it right!**
52. **Don't misinterpret.**
53. **Don't vacillate.**
54. **Be wholehearted.**
55. **Examine and analyze.**
56. **Don't wallow.**

**57. Don't be jealous.**

**58. Don't be frivolous.**

**59. Don't expect applause.**

**Keep a single intention.**

The *intention* referred to here is to be kind, to benefit others. It's the intention we began with, the intention we have adhered to. Don't be stuck on yourself. Consider others. Others includes oneself. One's self includes others. All activities should be done with this spirit, this sense of concern for others. When you eat breakfast, keep that spirit; when you go to the toilet, keep that spirit; when you walk upstairs, walk downstairs, cross the street, leave the house, come back into the house—keep that spirit. May I have breakfast this morning to nourish all beings. May I go to the toilet this morning to purify all beings and free them from what's inside that is extra and should be eliminated. May I walk up the stairs to rise up in goodness with everyone, walk down the stairs to deepen my commitment to truth for the benefit of others, leave the house to go forth to do some good for someone else, and return home in the hope that all beings will one day return to their true home. Whatever we do, we do unselfishly, with the spirit of dedication of our activity to others. This can be a creative practice. You can compose little sayings for yourself like the ones I've just suggested, and you can say them before eating (what's grace before meals, if not a version of this practice?), when going to the toilet, and so on; or more simply, and without words, pay close attention when you do these things, be really present for them, and conceive of your presence not just as yours and private but as inclusive of others— which, in fact, it is.

Can you actually sustain a practice like this? Of course not! You should have no expectation of becoming a saint with your mind constantly focused on concern for others. But to conclude from this that you might as well not practice **Keep a single intention,** since it is impossible, is also incorrect. You can practice it as often as you remember, and the more you practice it, the more you will remember. It's not impossible to have a practice of grace before meals. Millions have done so over the generations. And if you can practice grace before meals, you can practice "grace" at other repetitive occasions during the day.

### Correct all wrongs with one intention.

**Correct all wrongs with one intention** means that when we notice, inevitably, that we are not being so generous or so kind or so openhearted, that our activity has not been dedicated, in our hearts, altruistically, that instead we've completely lost track of all of our good intentions and have become, as if half-asleep, narrow, grim, and desperate, we should take a breath right there at the moment of noticing this. With that breath we forgive ourselves ("Oops, there I go again, sorry") and go on. We reset the dial with one intention: our purpose is to be of some benefit to others, to dedicate ourselves to others. This one intention is something that we can always trust and always rely on to set us straight, no matter how mixed-up we may be. Even when our motivations seem entirely false—when it seems that our wanting to meditate, our wanting to be good or wise, is completely self-serving and foolish or that we have stopped wanting to do anything spiritual whatsoever and we are completely lazy and sour—there is never any doubt about this single simple thing: yes, we do want to be of some benefit to others. Even when nothing else makes sense, this makes sense. Whatever is going on, always come back to this best and most basic motivation—the wish to care about others and to be of some service to them.

**Begin at the beginning, end at the end.**

**Begin at the beginning and end at the end** refers to a very practical and straightforward practice that I recommend to everyone. It's quite simple. At the beginning of the day, on arising, say to yourself (and you can train your mind to cue itself to the practice as soon as your feet first strike the floor on arising from bed): "Today I want to dedicate myself, to the best of my ability, to being generous and openhearted and benefiting others." That's the point of today. That's why you are getting up and not staying in bed. That's why you are going to work or doing whatever it is you are doing. If you are a daily meditator, you can then go on and practice meditation in this same spirit.

At the end of the day, before going to bed, perhaps sitting on the edge of the bed or getting into the bed, take a few moments to review the day's activities. Let your mind lightly slide over events that occurred, moments that will pop into your mind when bidden. And say to yourself, "May everything that I have done today, with whatever level of skill or good intentions, be dedicated to benefiting others. May my actions of today in some way be for the benefit of others."

The biggest problem with the idea of doing spiritual practice in our contemporary world is that there doesn't seem to be time for it. No time to meditate at home in the morning—must rush off to work. No time to meditate in the evening—too tired and, anyway, there's family, meals, more work, e-mails, phone calls. Certainly no time to go to a retreat, no time to go someplace to meditate with others—my schedule won't permit it, it is too expensive, too far away, and so on. This may all be true. But certainly there is no one who can't afford or is too busy to have a thought in the morning and a thought in the evening. Cultivating the discipline to practice this slogan, even if it is the only one you can manage to practice, is sure to have a big impact on your life. It will change the way you feel about your days and how you view them. You have been going through your life with some underlying attitude. Probably you don't even know what it is. But it conditions how you feel about your life. Practicing this slogan will ennoble and elevate that attitude. And that change of attitude will begin to affect everything in your life.

**Be patient either way.**

We've already contemplated the importance of the practice of patience or forbearance, which is not resignation or passivity but instead a strong endurance that has the effect of making us stronger and wiser. "Either way" reminds us that we have to practice patience not only when things are tough but also when they are not. If things go well, be patient, they'll change. If things go badly, be patient, they'll change. Don't get caught in your complacency when things are going well. If you can keep that in mind, then you probably won't lose it so easily when things go badly. The two go together. Receive whatever happens with as even a mind as possible.

Once upon a time there was a kindly Zen priest living in a temple on top of a mountain. One day there's a furious knock at the gate. A man and a woman are holding an infant, screaming at this priest as soon as he opens the gate: "A priest indeed! You are a disgrace to the Buddha Way! Our young daughter tells us this baby is yours. Take it!" The priest says, "Oh, is that so, is that so," and receives the child. The irate parents leave. Time goes by. The girl finally confesses to her parents that her pregnancy had had nothing to do with the priest; the father of the child is a young man from an important family, and not wanting to dishonor him or his family, she had blurted out that the priest was to blame, and now she is deeply regretful of this lie. The chagrined parents rush up to the temple and bow, bringing their heads to the floor. "We're so sorry. We can't believe we said those things, please forgive us." The priest says, "Oh, is that so, is that so," and returns the child.

This is how he practiced **Be patient either way.**

**Observe, even if it costs you everything.**

Traditionally, **Observe, even if it costs you everything** has to do with observing your religious commitments no matter what the cost, that is, keeping Buddhist or other religious vows that you have taken. In Zen we have such vows. The Three Refuges (which are common to all schools of Buddhism) are: taking refuge in Buddha as your teacher, Dharma as your teaching, and Sangha as your community. In the widest sense—which is how we understand them in Zen—this means committing yourself to the possibility of spiritual awakening, to the path of awakening, and to the community of all beings within which your awakening unfolds. The Three Refuges are one set of vows. In Zen we also commit ourselves to another set of vows, called the Four Bodhisattva Vows (I have already mentioned these earlier). These commit us to the necessarily impossible tasks of saving all beings, overcoming all delusions, mastering all positive practices, and becoming the practice, through and through. All very lofty and idealistic commitments, indeed. And yet they define the horizon of what's possible and what we aspire to, in the most noble and uplifting version of our lives. This slogan reminds us of them and urges us to keep to them, no matter what.

But for our purposes we can think of the word *observe* in a more open sense as simply to pay attention. All vows are included in this one commitment: to be committed to paying attention to our lives, to being honest about what is going on and unflinchingly realistic about how we are behaving and thinking. The heart of mind training is here: don't go to sleep, don't deny, don't make excuses, don't blame anyone, don't wish for something else. Live your life with your eyes and heart wide-open. No matter what.

**Train in the three difficulties.**

**Train in the three difficulties** is a slogan to keep us engaged with working on our various default habits, those unsuccessful yet compelling attitudes, thoughts, and actions that seem to keep coming back, over and over again, despite our best intentions. The first difficulty is when the habitual impulse first appears in your mind, the moment when it first pops up. Can you notice it? The second difficulty is that once it appears, it is compelling and very difficult to let go of. Can you let go? The third difficulty is that even if you can let go, it is hard not to be compelled by it all over again when it pops up again next time because of the force of the residual habit energy that you've been putting into it all of this time. Can you let go again and again, with patience?

To **Train in the three difficulties** would be to be able, first, to identify the habitual impulse when it arises; second, to let go of it once you recognize it; and third, to keep going with the first two so that eventually it won't come up again. This is easiest to practice on your meditation cushion when there's nothing else going on. You can notice painful or nasty states of mind arising, you can see that they are unnecessary and unpleasant and let them go by coming back to the feeling of the breath and the body as a substitute, and you can keep on doing this.

During the rest of the day, when life is a lot more complicated, you can use a simple three-step program. Step 1: notice when habitual negative thinking arises. Step 2: stop. Literally stop for a moment: if you are walking, stop walking; if you are sitting, stand up; if you are thinking, stop thinking. Step 3: take a breath. Return to awareness with that breath. This simple three-step practice is surprisingly powerful and can be applied to any slogan you are working with.

As we've said so many times, the slogans do not require us to be perfect. Quite the contrary, they recognize that the mind is extremely difficult to train and that mostly the training will proceed from failure to failure. But this is normal, that's how it works. So noticing that you are in a mess and being able to simply stop right there (without the frustration and recrimination taking over) and take a breath, and then with that breath returning to positive intentions—and being willing to do this time and time again as normal life—that's the essential practice.

### Take on the three principal causes.

Of the three principal causes, the first is *Find a good teacher*. No one can do mind training alone. The training implies a community of friends to commiserate with and encourage you and a guide or guides to help. Community is crucially important for our lives. We all crave it, even though it goes against the grain of our heroic can-do frontier spirit, which we persist in believing in, even in a global world. This spirit of self-reliance is good. Yet community remains essential. No one can live without it. In times gone by, community meant neighbors and coreligionists; these days community is both narrower and much broader and more various than that. Community is less built-in than it used to be and is more dependent on our own initiative and choice.

Teachers are an important part of our community. It's not important that our teachers be great or enlightened; in fact, having a great or an enlightened teacher can sometimes be a disadvantage. The point is to find a teacher you can actually work with, a teacher who can actually help you. In these days of Internet and long-distance travel, many people have teachers whom they seldom see or maybe have never met. One way or another, we can find the help we need. That is the first of the three principal causes.

The second principal cause is *Realize how important it is for you to tame your mind.* Recognize that mind training is not optional, it is essential. Everything in your life depends on it. Your job, your family, your relationships all depend on your maintaining a stable, buoyant, and kind mind. If your mind were to become dark and unstable, everything would fall apart.

The third principal cause is *Realize you have what you need.* You are alive, you have consciousness, you live in a world with others, you have the motivation to live a good life, you have food to eat and a roof over your head. What else do you need?

To practice this slogan is simply to recall all of this when you get grumpy or dissatisfied: remember your community and teachers, remember the importance of mind training, remember that you have what you need to do it.

**Don't lose track.**

**Don't lose track** of the three principal causes.

**Keep the three inseparable.**

The three principal causes are inseparable from one another. Your teachers and community evoke your intention to train, and your intention to train keeps them close to you. Your knowing that you have what you need reminds you that you want to keep on training to protect and extend your life to benefit others, and this desire keeps you in touch with your community and makes you appreciate more and more each day that you are living a life not of lack and need but of fullness. This feeling makes you want to share your life with your community more and more.

**Train wholeheartedly, openly, and constantly.**

**Train wholeheartedly** means with your full spirit, with all of your joy and all of your sorrow and all of your passion, leaving nothing out. **Train openly** means without hiding or favoring anything. Recalling that there's absolutely nothing to be ashamed of, nothing you need to hide, that everything in you can be brought forth at the proper time and all of it is not only worthwhile, it is all a necessary part of the picture. **Train constantly** means all the time, awake or asleep, in an energetic or a lethargic mood, when resting or having fun or being in a pickle: no matter what is going on, it is all in the service of mind training.

**Stay close to your resentment.**

Suddenly, and oddly, **Stay close to your resentment** pops up here in the midst of so many positive and inspiring reflections. Probably to remind us yet again that there is no escaping human problems, most of which come not so much from situations and other people as from our reactions to situations and other people. Among these reactions is resentment, which automatically takes us outside ourselves, leaping over our minds and what is going on in them to highly uncomplimentary evaluations of situations and other people—evaluations that make us feel tied up in knots. Resentment is a nasty feeling.

Despite that, this slogan tells us to **Stay close to our resentment.** Usually when we feel resentful, we are fairly convinced that we are beyond the pale, that our training has fallen apart, that we are completely in a mess. But this slogan is telling you that resentment is the greatest of all meditation objects. Far from feeling entangled in it and frustrated with that entanglement, we should celebrate it.

Think about it. What is resentment, after all? What happens when you stop projecting outwardly (because we are always resentful of *something* or *someone* out there, even if it is life, or ourselves, as if we were outside ourselves) and turn around to look at the resentment face-to-face to find out what it is? What color is resentment? Is it green? Is it purple? Is it pink? Is it white? Is it black? Is it tall? Is it short? Is it fat? Is it thin? What happens when you investigate? Can you look resentment in the face and see what it is? Can you feel the feelings, watch the thinking, see your actions unfold?

The investigation of resentment and of all afflictive emotions is the most powerful and the most beneficial of all practices. The peace that we are all seeking is less than half as good as the investigation of resentment, anger, greed, fear, and so on. These are basic visceral, human emotions. They are our great treasure. So we should always stay close when they arise in us, so that we can meditate on them.

### Don't be swayed by circumstances.

As we have already noted, it's always something. If things go well, be patient, they will change. If they go poorly, be patient, they will change. What goes up will come down, what is low will be high later on. There is no end to the vicissitudes of life, as my father would always say, quoting someone. It's no good if we are blown back and forth by circumstances to the point of instability, so that we lose track of ourselves to the west when the wind blows us that way, and then to the east when it reverses course.

But I don't completely agree with this slogan. I think it is good to be swayed by circumstances, like a bamboo that is flexible enough to sway in the wind. Swaying is one thing, being uprooted another. Can we be swayed without losing our place? Swayed but with solid roots. Firm yet flexible—maybe that's a better slogan.

### This time get it right!

**This time get it right** sounds like a joke to me, and maybe it is. After all of this training (this is the fifty-first slogan, after all), it seems that we keep on getting it wrong. After all of this maybe we haven't really begun. All of those other times we had it wrong, but *this* time we're going to get it right! This time I'm really going to pay attention, really going to think of others, really going to soften my heart and remember to love myself and love others and really open up and take a look. Maybe never before, and maybe never again, but *this* time!

Of course this time is the only time. There's only ever this time, no other time. This time lasts our whole life through. No need to worry about the past or the future: just **This time get it right!**

**Don't misinterpret.**

**Don't misinterpret** may mean **Don't misinterpret** the slogans, but it may also mean **Don't misinterpret** what's going on in your life. **Don't misinterpret** what others are saying or doing, **Don't misinterpret** your own thoughts and actions. In the Indo-Tibetan tradition there's a commentary to this slogan that lists the six ways in which we are likely to misinterpret, but probably we are clever people and we could find many more than six ways. Like all the other slogans that say don't do this or don't do that, the joke is that the slogan exists exactly because we always do that which the slogan is telling us not to do. Misinterpretation is constant and inevitable. If, as we've said earlier, we can't ever really fully understand ourselves or others, and if we naturally go on imagining that we can, then we are certainly misinterpreting. Maybe the slogan actually means, When you misinterpret, as you inevitably will, know that you are doing this. And try not to build too tall and cumbersome a castle on the shaky foundations of your misinterpretation.

Here is how to notice when you are misinterpreting. When your spiritual practice is making you unhappy, when you feel grim or miserable about it, or on the other hand, when you are feeling happy about your practice and therefore quite arrogant and disapproving of others who are not as peaceful and holy as you imagine you are—when this is your situation, it is a sure sign that you are misinterpreting. Mind training will sometimes be difficult. But even when it's difficult, you will feel some joy in it. You are happy that you have the opportunity to do this, and there is a sense of generous acceptance of your life even when it is tough and even when you make mistakes, as you certainly will. You don't need to overdo the highs and lows. What is true in your own case is true for others as well. All inflation and disparagement is misinterpretation. You, others, and the whole wide world are as they are. There's nothing to interpret.

### Don't vacillate.

**Don't vacillate** tells us that we vacillate all the time, as did the sages of the past. Keeping this slogan in mind, we try our best not to get carried away with all the thinking that goes on in our minds telling us that we can't do this or that, that we're this way or that way, that others are like this or like that. When you find yourself vacillating, weaving back and forth in your mind with a decision or a viewpoint, and you don't know what to do about it, do this: Ask yourself the following questions: Is impermanence true or not? Is sickness, old age, and death true or not? Ask yourself these questions seriously and honestly. If, as I expect, you answer Yes, I am afraid so; impermanence, sickness, old age, and death are, unfortunately or fortunately, quite true and there is no getting around them, then I think you will straighten out quite quickly and realize that you do not need to be so persuaded by your vacillating mind, that you can just take a stand somewhere, somehow, because life goes swiftly by, and in the big picture of things there is nothing at all to be confused about, and there is no choice but to maintain a stable and kind mind no matter what, and that you can do this under any circumstances.

### Be wholehearted.

**Be wholehearted. Don't vacillate. Don't misinterpret.** Stay open. Stay kind. Pay attention. Don't forget. Don't worry. Don't complain. Feel your breathing and your heartbeat. Come home.

**Examine and analyze.**

We were just discussing teachers. But the best teacher of all is one's self. It's necessary that you be a good and intelligent teacher for yourself, that you have the capacity to talk to yourself reasonably and for the occasion, so when you are tied up in knots and your mind is raging and you are discouraged and troubled, you have the capacity to stop and think about your situation carefully. You can ask yourself, "Is this raging doing me any good? Is this complaining and hollering and bemoaning my fate helping the situation? Am I enjoying this?" The answer to all of these questions is probably no. Then, having answered, you can assess the situation: "Okay, this is what is going on now: a b c d inside, and a b c d outside. Can I change the external circumstances?" And when the answer is "Yes, I can," then do that, change the troublesome conditions. Stop all of your chatter in the mind and figure out what you can change and go ahead and change it. When the answer is "No, these circumstances cannot be changed," the question then becomes, what *can* you change? You can change your heart, you can change your mind, you can change your attitude. After all, what you are really telling yourself when you are raging and complaining and feeling victimized is: "Things are not as they are, things are as I see them and want them to be." Or "They are as they are and I won't accept them." Either way, you are in trouble. A moment of sober reflection will make that clear. But you might say, "Maybe so, but I can't change my mind; try as I might, I am stuck in this bad emotional state." Then you can tell yourself, "Well, maybe I need support, maybe I need help." Of course you need help, who doesn't? So find some support and maintain that support even when you don't need it so that it will be there for you when you do need it.

As I noted before, we all do our best to take care of our health, our home, our finances. We pay our bills, we make sure there is enough money in the bank, we are concerned about these things, we pay attention to them. Why wouldn't we take just as much care of our hearts and minds, of our inner lives, and see that this is just as real and just as important as—and even more important than—our health, our home, our money. Because if our heart is broken and our mind is unstable, our health, our home, and our money will be of little consolation to us. Supporting your spiritual friends or your local church or group is just as important, and in exactly the same way, as taking out an insurance policy on your house. An insurance policy on your house (if you are lucky enough to have a house) is a necessity because you have to protect your house. Ensuring that spiritual support is there for you when you need it (and you always need it) is just as necessary. And more: you could get another house if this one burns down. You could earn more money if you lose your money. But if you lose track of your heart and your soul, it is very difficult to find it again.

If you **Examine and analyze** your actual situation for what it is, you will see that all of this is true and you will know how to take care of yourself.

### Don't wallow.

To be sure, your situation is certainly grave. You are a temporary, vulnerable human being in a limited, vulnerable world, and not a day goes by when you are not, exactly by the measure of that day, closer to death, when you will lose absolutely everything that you hold dear. So, yes indeed, you are in a perilous situation. But so is everyone else. Rich or poor, fortunate or unfortunate, whether they won the lottery or lost all of their money, everyone is in a very tough situation.

When we are full of self-pity, it's not because we are in a vulnerable, difficult situation. It's because we think that we are the central person in the universe and that we are worse off than anybody else. We think we are suffering, no one else is. This is never true. It makes a lot of sense to feel sorry for yourself. You *should* feel sorry for yourself. I certainly feel sorry for myself. It's very sad, very difficult, being human. But the whole point of mind training is to promote, to the bottom of our hearts, down to our bones, even to the marrow, the understanding and the feeling that we are not alone in this sadly poignant situation. We are together in it with everyone else. And that makes it beautiful, and even joyful, no matter how hard it may get.

**Don't be jealous.**

As I've said, my wife teaches middle school. She tells me that middle school is a seething cauldron of jealousy. This makes sense because when we're middle school students we are just at the age of a new and disturbing kind of self-consciousness that makes us particularly concerned with our position in social groups. We are beginning to wonder about who we are and what our lives will be, so we are quite concerned with feedback we are getting from others about this. Who likes us and doesn't, who we like and don't like, becomes very important. This makes for a lot of jealousy and pettiness, and many tears and much pain.

This is not surprising. What is surprising is that we can be fifty or sixty or seventy years old and from time to time find ourselves back in middle school. We can feel the same passion and jealousy when someone else gets promoted or advanced or appreciated and we don't. This slogan helps us to recognize the silliness of all of this.

The best way to practice **Don't be jealous** is to practice the opposite of jealousy, sympathetic joy. Sympathetic joy is joy you feel when others have joy. It is your own joy, but it comes not when causes appear for joy in your life but when they appear in someone else's life. You see someone else being happy and you take delight in that person's delight. You are happy for the person and with the person. You take the other person's happiness and you say, "Oh, this can also be mine. I am going to celebrate this as if it were mine."

This practice can be cultivated quite deliberately. You can practice it imaginatively on your meditation cushion, thinking of someone you know and love who is happy, or you can imagine another's happiness and feel it as your own. You can practice it at other times too, keeping on the lookout for people who are or seem to be happy (a happy romantic couple passing by on the street) and feeling their happiness as your own. Practicing this way will definitely reduce your jealousy—not only will you feel jealousy less, but the precise occasions that in the past made you jealous will now make you happy. Now you don't have to wait until something happens to you that will make you happy. You can be happy when anyone else is happy, thereby not only decreasing your jealously but increasing your possibilities for happiness many times over.

**Don't be frivolous.**

How much time we waste on frivolity and silliness! In our contemporary world we have devised more and more novel and enticing ways to waste time; it is a big industry, maybe even the biggest industry. This slogan is not telling us to be dour individuals who don't know how to have fun. We all need to have some fun. We need fun just as we need food, water, exercise, and time to ourselves. Having fun might involve doing activities that are purposeless, like watching clouds or water pass by. Or playing games. But when you are having fun, have fun; pay attention, don't use the purposeless activity for the purpose of distracting your mind from your own or the world's pain. Actually, there is no activity that is not frivolous once in a while, and any activity, including meditation practice, can be frivolous if you want to make it frivolous.

**Don't expect applause.**

**Don't expect applause** is the final slogan, very appropriate.

Almost everything that we have ever done in our lives from the first day, when we noticed that when we did it Mommy and Daddy smiled at us, up until yesterday, when we were awarded the scientific prize at the conference—everything, or almost everything, we've ever done has been done for the applause. It wasn't about the money or the prestige or the good we might have been able to do for others. It was about the applause. The approval we sought from others that we internalized into our sense of self. The applause that reassured us that the dread we felt, that came from a feeling inside that ultimately our life did not matter, was not a true dread, that we could brush it aside. The applause helped us to do that.

So that even now, as we commit ourselves to mind training, even at this moment, when we contemplate the final slogan that caps our effort to become good and kind people, we can't help but do it for the applause. For the applause of Mommy and Daddy inside us, who we know will applaud us for all of this.

I suppose there's nothing wrong with this. It's good for us to give and receive applause. Parents have applauded their children throughout the generations—and have hurt their children when they have withheld their applause. Praise is a fundamental spiritual practice—we praise the Lord or the saints for their goodness. We praise the sun and moon for shining. But when we are too much looking for applause or, as this slogan says, expecting it, needing it to justify ourselves, we are in trouble. We have lost our sense of self, lost our center. Although we can enjoy the applause that we will probably receive for practicing it, we practice mind training not for the applause but because we know it is right, we know it is necessary, and anyway there is no choice. Are we applauded for breathing? Are we applauded for standing up, sitting down, looking at the sky? Actually, we are applauded for these things. When people applaud us for our wonderful achievements, really what they are applauding is not us and not those achievements. They are applauding life, they are applauding goodness, they are applauding their own lives, they are applauding the human capacity to appreciate something wonderful. So it's good when they applaud. Let them applaud, and we will graciously accept it, knowing what their applause really means. And when they don't applaud, when instead they scorn us or yell at us, when they are mad at us for our many mistakes, which we might not have even realized were mistakes, we will graciously accept this too, knowing that it is something we can learn from and make use of.

So **Don't expect applause,** don't expect scorn, don't expect anything except the unexpected, because that is always what happens, even when you expected it. If you look a bit more closely, what happens is not what you expected. It's always something else.

# Afterword

In *Soul Mountain*, Gao Xingjian's great novel of contemporary China, there's a powerful passage about the death of a Buddhist monk in a remote mountain monastery. A great holy master, this monk had been preparing to die for a long time with special mediations and observances. When the day finally came, the mountain passes were thronged with people coming to pay their last respects. They listened respectfully to the old monk's final sermon (a brief paragraph in Gao's book), but it was incomprehensible to everyone, including the thousand or so monks who lived in the monastery. But so renowned was the old monk's religious power that crowds of peasants pushed forward for a last glimpse, and somehow, as the funeral pyre was lit, the crowd got out of control, causing a conflagration that burned down the monastery completely, destroying many lives in the process.

This is an image of religion at its most lurid and most powerful. Its mysteries inspire great faith, great passion, and great destructive force. The holy saint's sermon was incomprehensible. Even the monks couldn't understand it, and the monastery burned down to the ground. The master's miraculous powers became a memory, since there was no one to whom he could pass them on.

In old China (and in the Western world too) religion was like that: a precious and arcane tradition guarded by sacred elites. The people didn't understand it and didn't expect to. Their lives were crushingly difficult, and it was faith and devotion to their religion that gave them hope for a better world to come.

Now most of us want and expect better lives. And we aspire to develop greater understanding of ourselves and of the universe. We don't want to abandon hope in this world for hope in a world to come.

My life has been dedicated to finding a way to practice religion, serious religion—at least as serious as that practiced by sages of old—that speaks to our contemporary condition. If we are now facing hard times (as human being always have), much better to face them with patient compassionate hearts than with fear and panic. We have always needed one another. Our love for one another is both natural to us and something we need to strengthen through cultivation. We need sermons we can understand and use. We need many reminders and encouragements. I hope this book has helped.

# Appendix 1

*Seven Points and Fifty-Nine Slogans for*
*Generating Compassion and Resilience*

8. Begin sending and receiving practice with yourself.
9. Turn things around (Three objects, three poisons, three virtues).
10. Always train with the slogans.

### POINT THREE
## Transform Bad Circumstances into the Path

11. Turn all mishaps into the path.
12. Drive all blames into one.
13. Be grateful to everyone.
14. See confusion as Buddha and practice emptiness.
15. Do good, avoid evil, appreciate your lunacy, pray for help.
16. Whatever you meet is the path.

### POINT FOUR
## Make Practice Your Whole Life

17. Cultivate a serious attitude (Practice the five strengths).
18. Practice for death as well as for life

### POINT FIVE
## Assess and Extend

19. There's only one point.
20. Trust your own eyes.
21. Maintain joy (and don't lose your sense of humor).
22. Practice when you're distracted.

### POINT SIX
## The Discipline of Relationship

23. Come back to basics.
24. Don't be a phony.
25. Don't talk about faults.
26. Don't figure others out.

27. Work with your biggest problems first.
28. Abandon hope.
29. Don't poison yourself.
30. Don't be so predictable.
31. Don't malign others.
32. Don't wait in ambush.
33. Don't make everything so painful.
34. Don't unload on everyone.
35. Don't go so fast.
36. Don't be tricky.
37. Don't make gods into demons.
38. Don't rejoice at others' pain.

POINT SEVEN
## Living with Ease in a Crazy World

39. Keep a single intention.
40. Correct all wrongs with one intention.
41. Begin at the beginning, end at the end.
42. Be patient either way.
43. Observe, even if it costs you everything.
44. Train in three difficulties.
45. Take on the three causes.
46. Don't lose track.
47. Keep the three inseparable.
48. Train wholeheartedly, openly, and constantly.
49. Stay close to your resentment.
50. Don't be swayed by circumstances.
51. This time get it right!
52. Don't misinterpret.
53. Don't vacillate.
54. Be wholehearted.
55. Examine and analyze.

56. Don't wallow.
57. Don't be jealous.
58. Don't be frivolous.
59. Don't expect applause.

# Appendix 2

## *Basic Zen Meditation*

Basic Zen meditation is my own main spiritual practice. It is radically simple and easy to do. I have been doing it all of my life, and I recommend it to everyone. It makes no difference whether you are a Zen practitioner or ever intend to be one. Whether you are a Christian, a Jew, a Muslim, a Buddhist, or a secular humanist, this simple practice of sitting down and feeling the present moment of your living will have a powerfully positive impact on your life if you devote yourself to it. This practice serves as a background and basis for everything I have said in this book, and the book's message will be much more effective for the reader who, at least during the time of reading, takes it up on an experimental basis. Twenty or thirty minutes a day, best in the morning, before your day has begun and your mind's wheels have started turning quickly, will be enough. Less can also be okay.

The basic Zen meditation practice is called zazen (literally, "sitting meditation"). Probably most readers will be familiar with some version of it. It involves sitting up straight on a chair or a meditation cushion while paying attention to your breathing.

If you sit on a chair, it is best to keep your feel flat on the floor and to sit evenly on the seat without using the back of the chair for support, if this is possible for you. It is easier if the chair is not too soft. On a cushion (there are several types of meditation cushions available; a Zen meditation cushion is round and filled with buckwheat or kapok) you fold your legs in one of several positions: full or half lotus (one or both feet in your lap); Burmese (both feet flat on the mat or rug); or crossed ankles, tailor style (though this is not quite as good because your knees tend to float in the air; having both knees on the mat is more stable). You could also set the cushion on end, tall-wise, and sit as if the cushion were a horse, with your legs to either side of it, knees and shins on the mat or rug. Or you could use one of the many meditation benches now on the market at yoga stores or online. The bench will enable you to sit stably with your legs tucked underneath the seat.

Once you have figured out (for now, anyway) the best way to work with your legs, sit up straight on your cushion or chair (unkinking and lengthening the spine is an important factor in promoting alert awareness; relaxing too much makes you sleepy). This puts you in a posture of full human dignity, and just sitting in this way will promote awareness and a sense of your own nobility.

I think of this sitting up straight as "allowing yourself to be lifted from within." The point is not to willfully impose a rigid posture but, rather, to allow your body to be uplifted, letting this natural opening occur. To help this along, gently rotate the pelvis forward (this works whether you are on a chair or a cushion), which will arch the small of the back slightly inward. Let the back of your head float up toward the sky, the shoulders square, the heart area open up. This should feel like a gentle lifting, not a martial rigor. Tuck your chin in a little, so your nose is not pointing at the clouds.

Once you have found a balanced, upright posture, begin to pay attention to how your body feels as it sits. First, feel the pressure of your rear end on the chair or cushion. Notice the feeling of being supported from below—literally. The chair or cushion supports you, the floor supports it, and the earth supports the floor: you are literally being supported by the earth when you sit. Now you can concretely feel that support and entirely release your weight to it. Your weight is actually the index of the earth's supporting you. In pure outer space you don't weigh anything.

Next feel other parts of your body sitting: notice your neck and head and facial muscles; notice your shoulders and arms, your hands, your spine, your chest, your heart area. For the classical Zen hand position (*mudra*), **place the back of the left hand in the palm of the right,** with the hands held in the lap, gently curved, thumb tips gently touching. The arms are loose at the sides, not rigid or tight. They form a kind of oval. Holding the hands and arms in this way gives an alert, gentle, balanced focus. Sitting with balance, awake and yet relaxed, is key.

Now begin to pay attention to your breathing as it rises and falls in your lower belly. There's no need to create a special breath. Just be attentive to whatever breath appears—in, out, rising, falling. Usually just paying attention changes the breath slightly, making it a little slower and deeper. If it helps, you can count each breath on the exhale, lightly, from one to five, beginning again at one when you are done—or when you lose count. If you don't want to count, or if you get tired of it, you can just follow the breath as it comes in and goes out at the belly. If you get dreamy or lost, counting again will help.

Zazen is, fundamentally, sitting with the basic feeling of being alive. What is the basic feeling of being alive? Being conscious, embodied, and breathing. That is actually what it feels like to be alive. Every moment of your life, and all of your feelings, thoughts, and accomplishments, depend on this, but most of us hardly ever notice it. In zazen our task is just to be present with this and nothing else. Simply sitting aware of the feeling of being alive.

Of course, a lot of other things are going on when we sit in zazen. There are thoughts, feelings, memories, sensations, complaints. None of this is a problem or a mistake. The important thing is simply to return to the primary commitment—paying attention to the breath and the body—as soon as we notice we have forgotten about it. It's good to notice what has drawn us away, to appreciate it, and to remember that it is just exactly what had to be happening in that moment. But in this moment we come back without further ado. No tears and recriminations. We just come back to the feeling of being alive in the body and the breath. And there we are.

While there is much written and discussed about Zen and Buddhist meditation, and there are many specific techniques beyond this simple practice, meditation more or less does come down to this very basic practice. Essentially, it is nothing more than sitting with an honest awareness of the process of your life. While such awareness may seem exactly like the self-consciousness we usually feel in daily living, zazen practice will show us that it is in fact subtly but crucially different in that it is nonjudgmental and all-inclusive. This nonjudgmental and all-inclusive awareness, promoted and developed by meditation practice but more than meditation practice, will help us eventually understand and put into practice the wisdom and flexibility to deal with the events of our lives, and with others, that the slogans of this book suggest.

So this is the basic practice. We establish it always at the beginning and the end of our practice session. In the middle we might contemplate other things—in this case, whatever slogan we want to be working on. But we always maintain the attitude of basic mindful presence and gentle focus, without pressing and without blame.